Seeking Spiritual Beauty

Sheila Keckler Butt

Publishing Designs, Inc.
Huntsville, Alabama

Publishing Designs, Inc.
P. O. Box 3241
Huntsville, Alabama 35810

Second Printing, 2004
Third Printing, 2006
Fourth Printing, 2010

Publisher's Cataloging-in-Publication Data

Butt, Sheila
Seeking spiritual beauty./Sheila Butt
100 pp; 22.86 cm.
Includes Scripture text, beauty statistics, thought questions.
1. Women—Spiritual life. 2. Beauty
I. Butt, Sheila II. Title.
ISBN 0-929540-26-3
248.8

Printed in the United States of America

Contents

Introduction

"Blessed are the pure in heart, for they shall see God." — Matthew 5:8

In recent years bookshelves have been replete with books for women on how to become one's authentic self. There are books telling us how to live simply and abundantly. There are books telling us how to be content as women, wives, and mothers. There are books telling us how to find inner peace and spiritual renewal.

I have read many of these books and some of them offer a few helpful suggestions for simplifying one's life. Many times, however, these books leave the astute reader with a sense of searching and insecurity because they offer no definite answers for eternity. I find myself consistently returning to the one Book that endows and empowers us as women with the virtues that will guarantee all of these things if we are willing to live lives of commitment and courage in Christ. The Bible tells us that in Christ we have been given "all things that pertain to life and godliness" (2 Peter 1:3).

When we get into Christ our *destination* changes. We know that we can go to Heaven for eternity. However, in this life, when Christ truly gets into us, our *destiny* changes. We want to be like Christ. Our choices change. Our goals change. Our relationships to our God, our family, and other Christians change because we choose to emulate Christ. Rahab and Esther, as well as many others, changed their destinies by the choices they made after listening to what God would have them to do.

If this book is studied with a pure heart, it will change your life. A pure heart is one that is true to God and has a genuine willingness to see oneself as He sees us. The Bible tells us that the pure in heart will see God. The pure in heart are simply those who read the Word of God in order to find out what He has to say to us instead of trying to justify our personal opinions by taking verses out of context.

The discoveries you will find in the pages of this book may make you wonder for the first time in your life if you look like a gold ring in a pig's snout to our Lord (Proverbs 11:22) or if you really are seeking to be a spiritually beautiful person.

A sports commentator was discussing the deaths of Mickey Mantle and Dale Earnhardt and asserted passionately to viewers that God truly does have a special place in Heaven reserved for heroes. I could not agree more. The Bible tells us that "precious in the sight of the Lord is the death of His saints" (Psalm 116:15). He has gone to prepare a place for heroes. However, the heroes of this world and the heroes of faith have an entirely different agenda. The beautiful people of this world and the beautiful people of the Lord have an entirely different adornment. Ultimately, the heroes and the famous people of this world may not have their names written in the Book of Life.

It has been said that one can become so spiritually minded that she can be of no earthly value to the Lord. For many years, I wondered how that could be true. I know now. I understand that the most spiritual, most reconciling, most loving act ever committed on our behalf was also the most humble, humiliating, horrible experience that a person could ever endure. You see, the spiritual must be manifested in this physical world. If you want to know how to become a spiritually beautiful person, be prepared to learn some hard lessons. Whining women do not show the world the strength, character, and beauty of Christ. Each one of us has been put on this earth for such a time as this. As you begin the journey to spiritual beauty, be prepared to make some changes every day as you grow more into the likeness of Christ. Let's look into the mirror of His Word.

Chapter 1

The Eyes of the Beholder

> "If then you were raised with Christ, seek those things which are above, where Christ is, sitting at the right hand of God. Set your mind on things above, not on things on the earth." — Colossians 3:1–2

The most popular topic on which I have been asked to speak to Christian women over the past five years is *Seeking Spiritual Beauty*. This is not surprising in a culture that literally demands that women strive to be beautiful no matter what the cost physically, emotionally, or monetarily. I have a dear friend who has spent thousands of dollars on laser karitonomy, breast augmentation, phen fen diet pills, various surgeries, beauticians, expensive jewelry, and exercise equipment to make herself look beautiful. Her own mother told me recently that my friend would spend the rest of her life fighting her age and her weight. It saddens me to think that women in our society are so hopelessly obsessed. If beauty truly is in the eye of the beholder, then who are we really trying to impress?

The sincere desire to be spiritually beautiful in the sight of God will make you take a good long look into the mirror of your soul. You might be surprised by what you see. Are you spending more of your time and efforts looking into the mirror of the culture and trying to be beautiful and successful by the standards of the world, or are you looking into the mirror of the Word of God and understanding and trying to be what God would have you to be?

A young preacher was visiting with an older gentleman. While they were talking on the front porch, two dogs started fighting in the front yard. The young preacher thought one of them was really going to hurt the other and asked the old gentleman if they should not break up the fight. The old gentleman replied, "No. They do it all the time. I even know which one is going to win."

"Which one?" asked the young man.

"The one I feed the most!" laughed the old gentleman.

How true this is in our spiritual and physical lives. The life that shines through to the world and to our Father will be the one that we feed the most.

As you read this book, keep your eyes, as well as your heart, completely open to the possibility that some of the things you have always thought were important may be making you look like a "jewel in a pig's snout" to the Lord (Proverbs 11:22). What you can expect to gain from this study is not an expensive facelift—but a very precious "faithlift." It may last for eternity.

> *"But seek first the king-dom of God and His righteousness . . ."*
> —Matthew 6:33

We are a generation of seekers. We attend all kinds of workshops as we seek to learn new things, understand more things, or become something else. In the church today, we are very concerned about how to reach the "seekers" in the world with the Word of God, because we know that our culture is full of them. We are conditioned to believe that if we look long enough, pay enough money, make the necessary sacrifices, or invest enough time, we will get the things for which we are continually seeking.

A careful study of spirituality from the Scriptures will lead one to the conclusion that one cannot *find* spiritual beauty. It is not found at Weight Watchers or the Weigh Down Workshop. You can't take a pill and achieve it. You can't demand it. You can't buy it. You can't have a nice enough house or live in the right neighborhood to make you spiritually beautiful. You can't dress fashionably enough to command it. Spiritual beauty comes as a by-product of a Christian woman's life lived before the Lord in love and service to Him and to her fellow man. An ironic twist to spirituality (often defined in the dictionary as something unseen) is that it can be revealed only in the flesh. Our spiritual lives are not above the physical, but manifested by it.

The compelling evidence for this fact is made very clear in Matthew 25. Those people whom the Lord had separated to inherit the kingdom prepared from the foundation of the world asked Him,

> When saw we thee an hungered, and fed thee? Or thirsty, and gave thee drink? When saw we thee a stranger, and took thee in? or naked, and clothed thee? Or when saw we thee sick, or in prison, and came unto thee?

These people appear to be confused. They had been busy doing the Lord's work by taking care of those around them, regardless of the circumstances. They did not even realize that they were meeting the Lord and attending to Him every day while serving their fellow men. They were beautiful to our Lord. Taking care of the needs of others was a way of life for them and they were going to be rewarded for eternity.

I have seen spiritual beauty in the face of an 87-year-old woman who has spent her life serving others in the name of the Lord. I have seen spiritual beauty on the face of a dental assistant in Honduras who was sponging blood from patients' mouths as the dentist pulled almost a thousand teeth in five days. I have seen spiritual beauty on the faces of young teen-agers who were joyfully scrubbing lice from hundreds of children's heads. I have seen spiritual beauty on the face of many Bible class teachers, and I have seen spiritual beauty sitting at the bedside of the terminally ill. I have seen spiritually beautiful women in every shape, size, form, and fashion. But they were all sisters bearing the likeness of Christ. They were all bought with the same blood: a blood that is spiritual and eternal—a blood that truly is "thicker than water." It is even more binding and precious than the physical blood we have inherited from our parents.

Christ's death on the cross was the most physical, painful, humiliating act imaginable, yet it was the most spiritual event that has ever taken place. Had Christ not suffered that physical anguish and cruel injustice, we could not be reconciled to God. When we try to become so spiritually minded that we cannot touch, cry with, or joyfully serve those around us, then spiritual beauty is beyond our reach. We are like salt which is never poured out of the container. Stagnant salt cannot add taste nor does it preserve anything. It does not make people thirsty. It is useless. Eventually it loses its savor and has to be discarded. So it is with the stagnant Christian life. It tends to lose its savor and eventually becomes useless.

The spiritually beautiful woman is salt and light and leaven. She makes an impact on the world through service. She leads by modeling Christ. She gives her head, her hands, and her heart to serving others. Just as Christ willingly gave His hands to the cross and then His heart to those who crucified Him by saying, "Father, forgive them," the spiritually beautiful woman wills herself to give her hands and her heart to the work of the Lord. She becomes one of God's glory goals. It is through her life, her actions, and her character that others see Christ, and God is glorified.

Questions for Discussion

1. How can we take a good long look into our soul? By what should we determine our own beauty?

2. Why have we become such a generation of seekers? What is the most important thing that we should be seeking?

3. Why can't we find spiritual beauty?

4. Tell how we can compare ourselves to the faithful servants in Matthew 25? How do you suppose the world perceived their spiritual beauty and success?

5. Have you seen true spiritual beauty? When? What was happening?

6. Why does the author say that Christ's death on the cross was a spiritual act? Was it physically beautiful?

7. What does it mean to give your head, your hands, and your heart to becoming a spiritually beautiful woman?

8. How is the spiritually beautiful woman salt, light, and leaven?

9. How was Pharaoh used as a glory goal for God in Exodus 14:17–18? In a more positive way, how can the life of a spiritually beautiful woman be used as a glory goal for God? Is it her choice? What do we learn in Isaiah 43:7 about why we were created?

Chapter 2

⊙⊘⊘⊚⊙⊙

Our Adornment

"Do not let your adornment be merely outward—arranging the hair, wearing gold, or putting on fine apparel—rather let it be the hidden person of the heart, with the incorruptible beauty of a gentle and quiet spirit, which is very precious in the sight of God." — 1 Peter 3:3–4

When we are striving to please our God and Father in Heaven, we will not let ourselves be duped by the standards of our secular culture which is ruled and motivated by the media and by the great Duper himself, Satan.

In a survey of 33,000 women by *Glamour Magazine* in the early 1990s, the majority of respondents said that they would rather lose 10–15 pounds than any other goal in life. How shallow have we become? How many times have you stepped on the scales this month? This week?

"Charm is deceitful and beauty is passing . . ." worthy woman
— Proverbs 31:30

Today? Studies have shown that one of every four college-aged women has an eating disorder. In addition, a psychological study in 1995 found that three minutes spent looking at models in a fashion magazine caused 70 percent of women to feel depressed, guilty, and shameful.

When we spend more of our precious time on this earth dieting, exercising, and beautifying ourselves physically than praying, studying, and attending to the needs of others, then we have lost sight of true beauty in the eye of the most important Beholder.

A new clinic has opened this year in our area. It is called the "Youthful Image Salon." You can go there for every kind of beauty treatment or body enhancement. All kinds of surgeries can be performed. You are assured that you will leave there with a more youthful image. But don't be deceived—it is an image. It will not change your age, your character, or your destination for eternity.

Whatever the cost, physical beauty is corruptible. It will fade. The Christian woman should be much more concerned with the incorruptible, "even the adornment of a meek and quiet spirit, which is in the sight of God of great price" (1 Peter 3:4). In order to be pleasing to God, we will also adorn our lives with good works (1 Timothy 2:10). When we practice the presence of God and try to emulate Christ every day of our lives, it will not matter how much we weigh, what we own, or what we wear. Our true spiritual beauty will be reflected

> *"If anyone is in Christ, he is a new creation."*
> *—2 Corinthians 5:17*

in the faces and smiles of those whom we have served out of love. We will not be reflecting merely an image but rather a truth—the truth that only by seeking to serve others will spiritual beauty ever find us. Our countenance will reflect great joy and peace of mind in knowing that our Father will be beholding our beauty for eternity.

We are bombarded daily with advertising telling us how we can become more beautiful. If we use a certain product, weigh a certain amount, have a facelift, wear the right clothes, take the right medications, take enough vitamins, or attend the appropriate self-help seminars, we are being convinced that we can be beautiful. A young woman who has undergone approximately 40 operations to make herself look like Barbie was interviewed on television. Everywhere she goes, people tell her that she looks like Barbie. The commentator asked her if all of these operations were painful. She said that they were very painful, but she had accomplished her goal of looking like

Barbie, and therefore, the pain was of no consequence to her. This misguided young lady has led a dysfunctional life with a tragic prognosis. She will never be able to sustain her Barbie image, and underneath that image will be a famished soul.

In a similar vein, *USA Today* ran an article in February 2000 on fashion model Magali Amadei—one of our beautiful people, and often a role model for our young ladies—who has spent seven years bingeing and purging while suffering from bulimia. Stomach acids have eroded her teeth, resulting in 11 caps, seven root canals, and two bridges. She commented that she could very easily have severely damaged her intestines or reproductive organs. She described her life like this: "I would wake up every morning and think about when I would eat and throw up. I was constantly thinking about food and how fat I was." At one time she was bingeing and purging seven times a day and swallowing 40 laxative pills. She is 26 years old and says that she cannot even own a scale and risk weighing herself. It is too dangerous for her.

I personally know of a mother in her 40s who was not so lucky. She died of bulimia. She left two daughters in college and a 12-year-old daughter at home. She also left a loving husband. She was very active in her congregation and loved by the people there, but she never would admit that she had a problem and consequently no one could help her. Unfortunately, she bought in to the sick standards of our society and then found herself being controlled by them. Her body simply gave up and shut down after many years of abuse.

Time Magazine reported in January 2001 that anorexia and bulimia are becoming childhood diseases. The article points out that more than half of the boys and girls in first through fifth grades claimed to have dieted. Barbara J. Howard is quoted as saying:

> For children, it's stigmatizing to be fat. In one study, kids were shown pictures of overweight children and children in wheelchairs and were asked with whom they would rather be friends. They preferred the disabled children.

The article comments that "many children begin disliking their bodies even before they have started school."

People Magazine ran a story in November 2001 entitled "To Anorexia and Back." Unfortunately, one of the young ladies mentioned in the article is not making it back. She died of heart failure at the ripe old age of 25. The others who were interviewed still struggle daily with this monster after years of physically tormenting themselves. The article cited a study that shows that young girls are more frightened of being fat than they are of nuclear holocaust or of their parents dying.

In the past couple of years, I have begun conducting a seminar for young ladies on the topic "Made in His Image." This seminar emphasizes the worth of each young lady, as well as how precious and beautiful each one is, because she is made in the image of God. In this seminar we talk about the symptoms and causes of eating disorders. We talk about the pressure on young ladies to conform to the world. We

> *"It is no longer I who live, but Christ lives in me."*
> *—Galatians 2:20*

talk about dating and waiting and maturing in Christ. We talk about where these young ladies really live. Ask your daughter how many young people she knows who have, or seemingly have, an eating disorder. You will be amazed.

There are many good books at your local bookstore, and many good web sites, which will familiarize you with the signs, symptoms, and consequences of eating disorders. There is an enlightening book entitled *Reviving Ophelia* by Mary Phifer, Ph.D., which describes the agonizing dilemma in which the young ladies of our culture grow up today.

What a sad commentary on our society. We know that all of these attempts to sustain physical beauty are futile. Physical beauty will fade with age. It is destroyed by exposure to the sun. Spiritual beauty, on the other hand, becomes more glorious with age and is enhanced by constant exposure to the Son through the Word of God and our willingness to let the beauty of Jesus be seen in us. When we pattern our lives after Christ we know that we can achieve spiritual beauty for eternity.

Questions for Discussion

1. Why do you think Satan wants us to accept the shallow standards of our culture? What characteristics make him the "Duper"?

2. Why do we find it so hard to keep our adornment simple and pleasing to God?

3. What is meant by a "meek and quiet spirit" as discussed in 1 Peter 3? Does that imply that we are to be doormats? Look at this in light of 2 Timothy 1:7. How can we be powerful women with a "meek and gentle spirit"?

4. What are some of the comments we make or have made to our own children to make them start disliking their own bodies even before they start to school? How do we inadvertently let them know that we do not like imperfection? Shouldn't we, as Christians, be living by a different set of priorities?

5. What can each of us do to make a difference in some young lady's life? A second grader at a local elementary school recently wrote a short paragraph about her hero. As it turned out, her hero was my daughter-in-law. Why? Because my daughter-in-law never mentioned her being overweight! Are you some little girl's hero because you tell her that God loves her just the way she is? Do you really believe it about yourself? Pray and ask the Lord to give you a more perfect perception of beauty in His sight.

2 Timothy 1:7 For God did not give us a spirit of timidity, but a spirit of power, of love and of self-discipline,

(1 Cor 16:10 If Timothy comes, see to it that he has nothing to fear while he is with you, — — — because you

1 Tim. 4:12 Don't let anyone look down on you because you are young, but set an example for the believers in speech, in life, in love, in faith and in purity)

Chapter 3

๛๛๛๛๛

"What Women These Christians Have!"

"In like manner also, that the women adorn themselves in modest apparel, with propriety and moderation, not with braided hair or gold or pearls or costly clothing, but, which is proper for women professing godliness, with good works."

— 1 Timothy 2:9–10

It is to our advantage, as Christian women on our journey toward spiritual beauty, to pay close attention to history. The *International Standard Bible Encyclopedia* gives us insight concerning women in the New Testament church, through the eyes of the third-century historian, Tertullian:

He mentions the modest garb worn by Christian women as indicating their consciousness of their new spiritual wealth and worthiness. They no longer needed the former splendor of outward adornment, because they were now clothed with the beauty and simplicity of a Christ-like character. They exchanged the temple, theaters, and festivals of paganism for the home, labored with their hands, cared for their husbands and children, graciously dispensed Christian hospitality, nourished their spiritual life in the worship, service, and sacraments of the church, and in loving ministries to the sick. Their modesty and simplicity were a *rebuke to* and *reaction from* the shameless extravagances and immoralities of heathenism. That they were among the most conspicuous examples of the transforming power of Christianity is manifest from the admiration and astonishment of the first-century pagan Libanius who exclaimed, "What women these Christians have!"

The first thing Tertullian mentions is the modest clothing worn by the Christian women. He mentions modesty as being one very noticeable characteristic that set the Christian women apart from the women of the world almost immediately. One cannot help wondering if he would recognize Christian women that quickly today.

Are we set apart from the world by our modesty? When a contemporary Miss USA claims to be a strong Christian and yet parades herself in front of hundreds of thousands of viewers in an extremely immodest bathing suit, one has to believe that Christians have lost the battle on teaching modesty. At the risk of sounding old-fashioned and archaic, I can unreservedly tell you that I would not be proud of my Christian daughter (or granddaughter) for compromising her modesty for any reason. Can we really believe that our Lord considers immodesty a virtue? We must be very careful whom we extol as role models to our children. This is a prime example in which we often let the culture instead of the cross rule our lives.

We can rationalize almost anything as the best choice because some good might come from it. The popular song, "From a Distance," was written several years ago. The theme of the song was that God is watching us from a distance and that, from a distance, everything looks good to Him. I could not disagree more. As Christians we must understand that our Lord is present in our lives and that we are truly to imitate Him. He certainly knows if a thing is good or bad and shows us through His word how to discern good and evil. One aspect of spiritual beauty is living in the presence of God in every moment and hour of our daily lives.

When our three sons were in Christian schools, I was always amazed on "Banquet Night" that many of the beautiful, precious young ladies I had seen at school on any given day looked more like streetwalkers. They had been transformed by makeup, hairstyles, and often expensive, immodest dresses to look 10 years older then they were. It had become such a problem throughout the years, that finally, when my youngest son was invited to the banquet in his senior year, I heard him ask the young lady on the phone. "Is your dress modest?"

Another time at Freed-Hardeman University during their Horizons Program for young men and women, we had a panel of young men addressing a panel of young ladies. The young men were asked by the panel of young ladies what bothered them most about the young ladies. The young men unanimously answered, "The way you dress!"

The young ladies, of course, were shocked. They did not understand that men and women often see things differently. I believe that many Christian mothers do not understand this either. We tend to see our 14-, 15-, and 16-year-old maturing young ladies as still being our sweet, innocent little girls. We still think of them and see many of the clothes they are wearing as being cute.

Here is sound advice to mothers: If your husband questions your letting your daughter wear something out in public, don't let her wear it. Don't question him in front of her and don't insist that it just looks cute on her. Simply ask her to change in deference to her father's wishes. If you start early enough teaching modesty, confrontations on apparel selection will seldom be necessary. I am already pointing out immodest apparel to my three-year-old granddaughter and showing her what really looks pretty.

Recently we were looking at dolls and she wanted a "real" Barbie. Up to that point we had just seen imitations. A few minutes later she spotted a Barbie. "Oh Bebe! There is a real Barbie!" She picked up the box, looked at it and put it back on the shelf. "We can't get that one," she said. "She's not modest!" It occurred to me that if a 3-year-old could tell what is modest, why can't a 14-, 15-, or 16-year-old young lady or her mother?

> *"In like manner also, that the women adorn themselves in modest apparel . . ."*
> *—1 Timothy 2:9*

I was told many years ago by a spiritually beautiful woman to dress as if I wanted the men in the congregation to treat me as a sister. That has proven to be extremely valuable advice, and I am sure it has kept me from receiving much criticism over the years. It has allowed me to be of more service to my Lord, my husband, and the congregations that we have served.

One evening while he was working with a jail ministry, Dewayne Spivey make a poignant observation:

> It was Thursday night and I sat alone in the guard room of our local jail. My Bible class had finished early and I was waiting on the other groups to finish so we could leave together. Every person wishing to visit someone must pass through this room. As I waited I glanced over the signs that were posted to give visitors various warnings and cautions. One sign caught my attention because it was posted as least four times in key locations. All of the other signs were posted only once. Obviously this was a message they wanted to make sure all visitors understood. What message do you think a jail would want to make sure got across to its visitors? It wasn't about bringing in anything that could be used as a weapon. The sign read as follows:

> ATTENTION VISITORS

> No person admitted unless properly dressed.
> 1. Shorts must be knee length.
> 2. No tank tops.
> 3. No short dresses.
> 4. No sun dresses.
> 5. No shirts with obscene language or pictures.
> 6. No see-through clothing.
> Any person that cannot abide by these rules will be refused visitation.
> (No exceptions)

Spivey goes on to ask:

> Why would this be such an important notice to visitors of a jail? Obviously the administration was aware that the way someone dressed could have an adverse impact on the people they were charged with housing and controlling. They were aware of the problems that improper dress can create and they wanted to avoid them.

Spivey continues:

> Shouldn't Christians be even more concerned when it comes to the way they dress? Our dress is to portray an image of godliness. We should be concerned with the problems our dress may cause in the

minds of others. Should a jail atmosphere be more concerned with modesty than the person who is trying to exemplify the Christian life?

The truth is, dear sisters in Christ, that the way we dress is a reflection of our hearts and our inner spirit. The way we dress portrays whether we are striving for inner beauty or sordid attractiveness. The way we dress tells the world a lot about our souls.

We learn in Proverbs 2:11 that "discretion will preserve you; understanding will keep you." That may literally mean that discretion will keep you safe.

Let me share with you a letter that was written to Ann Landers illustrating the problem of immodest innocence:

Dear Ann,

First, you should know I am a happily married man, the father of two children. I work in the shoe department of a large store in a shopping center. I don't know what to expect next in the way of women's apparel.

It's not what they are wearing but what they are not wearing that bothers men. Middle-aged women as well as young girls come in with their bare midriffs, belly buttons winking at me through rolls of fat, breasts flopping around under flimsy halter tops, hip-hugger pants so low you are afraid to look for fear they might slip a quarter of an inch.

This afternoon, a girl about 17 came in with her father. I couldn't believe my eyes. She was built like Raquel Welch. There she sat in a see-through blouse with such an innocent look on her face. The blouse was so tight she was about to pop two buttons. If a guy had made a pass at her, the old man would have flattened him, yet that girl was a case of indecent exposure if I ever saw one.

Please tell the females out there that when they go in public half naked, they look like tramps.

Signed,

Happily Married

Is this young lady asking for trouble? She may not even realize it, but from a man's point of view, we learn that she is an accident waiting to happen. In 1 Timothy 2:9–10, Paul tells us to adorn ourselves "in modest apparel, with propriety and moderation; not with braided hair, or gold or pearls, or costly clothing: but which is proper for women professing godliness, with good works." Women who are seeking spiritual beauty will dress in such a way as to bring themselves honor, and not a second look from lustful eyes. To wear scanty, tight, or immodest clothing is an offense toward God and toward those around us whom we are inviting to sin. We do not have the right or freedom to wear what we choose and expect others to keep their eyes to themselves. We do not

> *"Let your adornment . . . be the hidden person of the heart."*
> —1 Peter 3:4

have the right to think everyone else just has a dirty mind. We cannot flaunt ourselves before the public and ignore Paul's directives to Christian women if we are really concerned about being spiritually beautiful. We need to understand that we are made in the image of God and that our bodies are the temple of the Lord.

We have already looked at Proverbs 11:22 which tells us that a beautiful woman without discretion looks like a gold ring in a pig's nose to our Lord. The word *discretion* here involves two areas of our lives: the way we dress and the words we speak. The woman who dresses in a provocative manner is being ruled by the prince of this world and saddens the Lord. She looks like a waste of beauty to Him. She looks like a gold ring in a pig's snout.

The importance of modesty will be even more relevant to us when we understand what is happening in our society. Many news articles have been written recently about our public libraries letting people log onto pornographic sites in the name of freedom of speech. The librarians admit that it is not healthy for the children who are in the library at the time, but they are opposed to censorship. Their solution is to have designated hours for logging on to the pornography. The cubicles are often not enclosed and one can easily see what is on the screen of a neighboring computer. Children under 18 are not allowed to log on to the sites, so during those particular hours the computers are controlled almost entirely by adult men. When time is up on one computer, they simply log on to another. Not only does this keep the computers tied up for those two or three hours a day, it is easy for children to see what is on the screen. It has been observed that children are watching the facial expressions of the voyeurs and hearing them make all kinds of strange sounds. Sometimes two or three men are standing around the computers.

I have a 56-page report by David Burt from the Family Research Council entitled *DANGEROUS ACCESS: 2000 EDITION, Uncovering Internet Pornography in America's Libraries,* which enumerates these findings and many more. Would you want your precious young daughter (or son) to walk into a public library during this time of day immodestly dressed? It's a frightening thought, isn't it?

We need to understand the reasons for the commands of our Lord. They are for our own good. A spiritually beautiful woman knows that and cultivates that attitude in her heart and in the hearts of those around her. She knows what is happening in the world and safeguards her family as well as those whom she may be teaching. There have been times when I have taught a young girls' class on modesty only to greet some of their mothers following the class who were scantily dressed themselves.

As Christian women, we need to take good, long, honest looks in the mirror. Look in your closet. Look at pictures of yourself. Reevaluate your wardrobe. Reevaluate your daughter's wardrobe. I often tell young ladies that if something is not on sale, they should not advertise it. Women who are seeking spiritual beauty will be advertising their goodness by the way they dress. What are the women in your family advertising? Are you showing the world that you are seeking spiritual beauty?

Questions for Discussion

1. Why does it help us to know what Tertullian wrote about the Christian women in the New Testament church?

2. Would someone be able to tell that we are Christians by the way we dress today? In the church building? In the mall? At the beach?

3. How do we often rationalize immodesty? (Example: "I am more modest than she is.")

4. Do you believe the man who wrote the letter to Ann Lander's made a truthful observation? How can older women help young girls who seem not to understand the danger of immodest dress?

5. Discuss the different viewpoints men and women have on modesty? How can we, as Christian women, dress like we are made in the image of God?

6. Do we have the right to wear whatever we want as Christians? Defend your answer. (Remember, we were bought with a price. Study 1 Corinthians 6:15–20).

7. Why would the administration of the prison be so concerned about modesty?

8. The Bible addresses modesty in several places. Do a personal study on modesty from the Scriptures. If you are in a class situation, you may want to share your study. Give examples of modesty and immodesty.

9. The Bible is not a rule book of "do's" and "don'ts" but a standard for the best Christian life possible. Many of its admonitions are for our own safety. How can we show this in our own lives and teach it to others?

10. Are we, in the Lord's church, losing the battle on modesty? How can we make a difference?

Chapter 4

၄၇

In His Image

"So God created man in His own image;
in the image of God He created him; male
and female He created them."

— Genesis 1:27

Do you not know that you are the temple of God and that the Spirit of God dwells in you? If anyone defiles the temple of God, God will destroy him. For the temple of God is holy, which temple ye are (1 Corinthians 3:16–17).

We need to make sure that young ladies in the church are taught and demonstrated the right priorities. We need to let them know that they are made in the image of God and that they are very special. We need to praise them for visiting the nursing homes and taking care of a young mother's children for her. We need to praise them for their modesty and their love and concern for others. And most of all, we need to be modeling spiritual beauty for them.

In studies of young women who have been involved in abusive relationships and dating violence, it has been discovered that the one thing that helps many of them get out of a bad situation is being told by someone that "you don't deserve this!" If a young lady knows that she is made in the image of God, she knows that she deserves the best life has to offer. Look around at our precious young ladies and you will see that many of them are settling for much less than they deserve. Why? It is because they have bought into the cultural ideals—which for 95 percent of them are unattainable—and think they are lucky just to have a boyfriend at all.

We learn in Proverbs 23:7 that "for as he thinks in his heart, so is he." That is true of all of us, and much of what our young ladies believe about themselves is a reflection of what we think of ourselves. A very pretty, average-sized young mother (did you know that the average American woman weighs 144 pounds and wears a size 12 or 14?) came up

> *"For as he thinks in his heart, so is he."*
> *—Proverbs 23:7*

to me after one of my presentations. She said, "When I got ready to leave this morning, my 8-year-old daughter looked at me and said, 'I'm going to be fat, just like you, Mom!'"

This young mother was not fat. She went on to say, however, that she often mentioned in front of her daughter how much she would like to lose weight. Consequently, the daughter believed that she was going to be fat.

I have read of cases of anorexic young ladies who had no physical or psychological reasons to be paranoid about their weight or eating habits. Many times the problem was traced to a mother who was overly concerned with her own weight and appearance.

Christian mothers, by their example, should begin teaching their daughters about spiritual beauty at a very early age. We need to understand that each one of us is made in the image of God. Even though we come in all shapes and sizes, we need to learn to be content and happy with our bodies, while keeping them as healthy as possible. We are all "fearfully and wonderfully made" (Psalm 139:14) and we need to be thankful for that blessing. Spiritual beauty will be much better caught than taught.

Also, we need to be very cautious about the comments we make to other people's children and our grandchildren. We don't need to constantly be telling them how pretty they look, or how pretty their dress is, or how perfectly their hair bow matches their dress. We need to be complimenting them on kindness, sharing with others, sweetness, and inner beauty. We ourselves need to reconsider the time we spend being concerned with how we look to the world. Do we spend more time in the bathroom mirror than in prayer and study of the Word of God which are the true mirrors of our soul?

As we exemplify spiritual beauty in our lives by our modesty, we are also to be examples to the believers in conduct and in purity (1 Timothy 4:12).

Here is an example of one mother who was able to do that:

> A young lady came home from college and was having a heart-to-heart talk with her mother. She mentioned to her mother that she remembered how her mother would have devotionals every afternoon, even while the daughter was in high school.
>
> "But how did you know that I was still doing that while you were at school," her mother asked.
>
> "Because when I came in from school in the afternoons I would see your Bible on the bed and your kneeprints in the freshly vacuumed carpet?" her daughter explained.

What a great legacy this mother was leaving her daughter. She was showing her daughter by her conduct that she was truly living a spiritual life. Her daughter, and most likely her grandchildren, will be blessed for it.

We also need to be examples of purity. In another instance, one of the school resource officers in our community was telling about his beautiful young daughter who had gone to college in another city. She came home and told her parents that her roommate had been teasing her about being a virgin. Her roommate often told her that she was the only virgin in that dorm and that she was being silly and old fashioned.

One night the young lady said that she had just had enough. As her roommate was walking out the door and making fun of her for her purity, she told her roommate, "I can go out and be like you any night that I choose, but you can never be like me again!"

Needless to say, this was a proud dad. He was telling this story to a group of young people to whom he was encouraging abstinence. Someone had exemplified and taught this young lady about purity, and her life will be blessed by that teaching.

A spiritually beautiful woman knows that purity before marriage is withholding herself from the man she loves in obedience to God and that purity after marriage is being responsive and giving herself to the man she loves in obedience to God. That is one of the reasons that older women are told to teach the younger women to love their husbands. Younger women do not need to be taught about lust. They do not need to be taught to get butterflies in their stomachs every time a certain young man walks into the room. But they do need to be taught, and have demonstrated to them, that true love is an act of will and is not based on our fleeting emotions.

> *". . . that they may admonish the young women to love their husbands . . ."*
> *—Titus 2:4*

Somewhere along the line in the church, we have missed teaching our young ladies *who* they are, *what* they are, and that they were made in the image of God. Older women are commanded by God to teach the younger women, but our response to this command has been less than enthusiastic. Possibly because we have been told so often that we are to "sit down and be quiet" in the church, we are afraid to teach anyone. That fear or unwillingness to teach on our part, as Christian women, is unbiblical, and certainly not spiritually beautiful.

I received this letter from a young lady after she had read an article I had written on "The Missing Ingredient of Titus 2."

> Having just finished reading your article on Titus 2 in *The Gospel Advocate*, I felt led to write and let you know what a truly awesome inspiration it was to me. As a freshman in college, I am sometimes overwhelmed by pressure of society to find success and contentment through a career and status in the "working world." I am so thankful that my mom made the decision to stay home and instruct me, through her loving example, [in] the role of a Christian woman. However, if it weren't for my mother, I don't know where else I would have been given the opportunity to learn and observe these essential traits and values. The majority of women within the church have failed to lead and teach us, the younger women, these key components that we are commanded by God to obey. Your article has both encouraged and challenged me to comply to and fulfill this role, given by the Lord in

Titus 2:3–5. It is my prayer that the Lord would use me to incite this desired obedience within other women also. The Lord has really used your words to speak to my heart.

Kara Craven

What about those young ladies who do not have godly Christian mothers? Are we just going to leave them to their own discretion? We must not abdicate or underestimate the responsibility we have for teaching younger women. We are commanded by God to teach them "to love their husbands, to love their children, to be discreet, chaste, homemakers, good, obedient to their own husbands, that the word of God may not be blasphemed" (Titus 2:4–5). Teaching these things to young women is another one of God's glory goals. He wants us to teach them in order that His word may not be blasphemed. In essence, He wants us to teach these things to them so that by their lives His word will be confirmed.

On the journey toward spiritual beauty our choices will determine our destiny and will be made in view of eternity. Our choices will be different from the choices of women of the world.

After my father died several years ago, I was visiting with a friend of my mother whom we had not seen for many years. She had come to the funeral from Illinois. When she saw me she exclaimed, "Sheila, I am so glad to see you. You know, I always thought you were going to grow up to be someone rich or famous one day, but here you are just a regular person!"

For a moment, I was surprised and hurt. And then I began thinking about the choices I had made since we had last met. Shortly after Stan and I married, I had chosen to become a Christian. Just a few months after that I had chosen not to take a part on the John Davidson television special for which I had been auditioning, because I was being asked to wear very immodest apparel. Later, I had chosen to stay home and rear my children rather than climb the corporate ladder. I had chosen to use my college education to enhance their intelligence. I had chosen not to change the world for my children, but to help change the world through my children. Stan and I had sold our home and our automobile dealership in Tennessee to attend the School of Biblical Studies in Denver, while our children were still very young. I realized upon reflection that my choices had determined my destiny and I had made them in view of eternity. I realized that I was truly happy just to be a regular person in the eyes the world. I knew that I was living an authentic life. I also realized I was laying up treasures in Heaven and that if my name was written in the Book of Life, I needed no other notoriety.

Questions for Discussion

1. Why is it so important for us to model spiritual beauty to our young ladies? In what ways can we show them that inner beauty is much more precious to the Lord?

2. If we are made in the image of God, why do 75 percent of women become dissatisfied with their bodies after looking at fashion models in a magazine for 10 minutes? Do Christian women react this way? Why?

3. Why are our young ladies settling for so much less than they deserve?

4. How might we as Christian women be able to help someone who is in an abusive situation?

5. What does Proverbs 23:7 say to us? How can we be helpful to others by understanding this principle?

   a. How can we encourage our Christian young ladies to keep themselves pure?
   b. Why is it so important to make our choices in view of eternity?
   c. What sometimes makes it hard for us to make our choices in view of eternity?
   d. Do you think there are any just "regular" people to the Lord? Explain your answer.

Chapter 5

⊙⊘⊙⊙⊛⊙

Open Heart, Open Home

"O Corinthians! We have spoken openly
to you, our heart is wide open."

—2 Corinthians 6:11

Do you realize that it is possible for your heart to be standing wide open and you are not having open-heart surgery? At least not physically. You may need some spiritual open-heart surgery, however.

The spiritually beautiful woman will live her life on this earth with an open heart and an open home. She will realize that her house, her apartment, her condominium, and her family belong to God and has been given to her to use in His service. There, she is to raise her own children to love the Lord.

A middle-aged woman was remorsefully discussing her unfaithful children with an elder in the Lord's church. She commented, "I don't know what went wrong. I raised them in the church!" The elder kindly looked at her and said, "Ma'am, you should have raised them at home and then brought them to church."

Shortly after our youngest son went away to college, he called home one evening. In the course of our conversation, he commented, "Mother, I didn't spend the night away from home much, did I?" I think it was just dawning on him that he had rarely spent the night away from home. There were two reasons for that. The first reason was that Stan and I made an agreement with each other when the boys were very young that we would never tell them that a friend could not spend the night. We kept this agreement to the very best of our ability. I don't ever remember saying that a friend could not spend

> *"Better is a dry morsel with quietness, than a house full of feasting with strife."*
>
> *—Proverbs 17:1*

the night. The second reason Kyle had rarely spent the night away from home was because most of our children's friends were at our house. With three boys, three years apart in age, there was always a party at our house. Stan and I intended for it to be that way. We often had to run to the store for food, or pack up and go to McDonald's. And yes, many times it was a strain on our budget. Sometimes we simply had popcorn and cold drinks. And I had a reputation for serving great grilled cheeses. It was something I could serve relatively cheaply and plentifully.

Just this past Mother's Day, I listened to Stan Jr.'s Sunday morning sermon on audiotape. He told the congregation that his mother was not a gourmet cook and that I was probably not even a really good cook. He told them that we had four or five standard meals that I cooked often. He mentioned spaghetti, chili, pot roast, and potatoes. I guess I should have been embarrassed. But he went on to say that what he remembered most was that he never had to call home and ask if he could bring a friend for dinner. He always knew there would be plenty of whatever it was.

Sometimes I wonder if we feed our visitors or if we feed our pride? Do we get too busy to enjoy the people in our home as people, or do we just see them as objects to be fed? The Bible tells us to "be hospitable to one another without grumbling. As each one has received a gift, minister it to one another, as good stewards of the manifold grace of God" (1 Peter 4:9–10).

I might not have the gift of cooking, but I am thankful that I have the gift of hospitality. It is a precious gift with great rewards in being able to turn ordinary hamburger or grilled cheeses into an extraordinary relationship with people. I am going to guess that you have that gift, too, if you are willing to focus on the people who come into your home rather than how you and your house appear to them.

Anne Ortlund, in her book *Disciplines of a Beautiful Woman*, says there are two kinds of women in the world: the kind who say, "Here I am!" and the kind who say, "There you are!" The woman who lives with an open heart and an open home radiates a welcoming, "There you are!"

During our children's high school years, we lived right across the railroad tracks from the school. We had made a conscious decision to live within walking distance of the school. It gave us a great opportunity to be available for the young people. Many times the various teams would come to our house before practice for a snack and some attention. Mothers would call and ask if their children could come to our house in case of an emergency or if the parent was late in picking them up from school. There were times when young people knocked on our door late at night because they knew we would be available. Sometimes it was a problem with their car, sometimes it was problem with their date, and sometimes they just wanted to come in and visit.

We did not have a large house, and I remember Stan and I trying to sleep many nights with the sound of bellowing laughter in the living room or upstairs. We lived in an older home, and I remember lying in bed thinking that surely one of those big boys was going to come through the ceiling the way they were playing around up there. As a matter of fact, Kyle and one of his junior high friends were exploring the attic one day and we did come home to find his friend hanging from a two-by-four over our dining room table. When Stan Jr. was describing this same young man recently, who is now a youth minister, Stan wrote: "John and I grew up together. There is not much that we haven't shot at, blown up, or set on fire at some time in our young lives!" (Thankfully, I didn't know everything at the time.)

When I was speaking at a ladies' retreat near our home some time ago, one of the ladies came up and told me: "I know the beds were not always made at your house. My son told me." I could only smile because I had precious memories of her son—an only child—piling up in those beds many nights with several other young men during his high school years.

The spiritually minded woman who opens her home to the world understands that her home is not just for her own comfort and the comfort of her family, although that is one very important aspect of it. Her home is the very reflection of her soul. Consequently, the home of the woman who is emulating Christ will also be a haven for those who have been wearied by the world.

> *"Be hospitable to one another without grumbling. As each one has received a gift, minister it to one another . . ."*
> *—1 Peter 4:9–10*

Her home will be a place of refuge from the culture.

I know a brother and sister, who are now older adults, who told me this about their home when they were growing up:

> Our mother was a meticulous housekeeper. You could eat off her floors. She was proud of her home. But when our daddy came in from working long hours in the factory, he was not allowed to lie on the bed because he might mess it up. We remember him lying on the hardwood floor beside the bed. We hate that memory to this day.

I had another close friend several years ago whose husband was a doctor. She had worked and helped put him through medical school. During that time they lived in a trailer and were extremely happy. When her husband began making lots of money—Elvis Presley was one of his patients—they bought a beautiful house in a very expensive neighborhood. After that, he often told us how much he dreaded Thursdays, because that was vacuuming day. He would have to take his shoes off at the doors and walk around the carpets so he would not mess up the nap of the freshly vacuumed rugs. This precious Christian couple divorced a few years later, and I could not help but wonder if it was because of her clean house but her messed up priorities. A spiritually beautiful woman will own her house and not let it own her. She will not let it interfere with her love for her family or her hospitality toward people in the world.

Although Jesus did not condemn Martha for her concern for the temporal things, He told her that Mary had chosen the better part. The spiritually beautiful woman will be more concerned with the better part. She will know the difference between a house and a home. She will understand that her house is the structure in which the family lives, but her home will be the life they live in the walls of that house. She will understand that her home and her family are all one unit working in service to the Lord. She will stress this to her children and exemplify it by teaching others about the Lord in her home. She will model this attitude by looking at every visitor as an opportunity instead of an intrusion.

> *"He blesses the home of the just."*
> —*Proverbs 3:33*

She will have a home which is focused on Christ-esteem rather than self-esteem, and those who enter her home will have no doubt about it.

The spiritually beautiful woman will inspire her children to teach others and to bring them into their home for encouragement. Her home will exemplify the New Testament sense of community in which the members eat together, play together, pray together, rejoice together, and suffer together. The family who loves the Lord will pray often and guests will be included. When it is time for Bible study or devotional, guests will be included. Never put off or neglect Bible study, prayer, singing, or devotions because you have company. If the company is young children, just include them. If it is adults, just tell them that this is your time together to study the Word and include them. Most of the time you will be pleasantly surprised by their reactions. Most people are encouraged to see that a family is living their beliefs. They will respect and admire your family and maybe even eventually, your God. Truly having an open heart and home does not consist of just a couple of hours a day. It is a way of life.

We need to practice unconditional love in our homes. It must be the same kind of love that Christ had for us. It is *agape* love and it will come with a price.

A little girl was praying in my preschool Bible class and she said, "Dear Lord, please let our hearts grow big." I thought how beautiful that was, and how scriptural. The Bible assures us that our hearts can be enlarged toward people (2 Corinthians 6:11). It is a matter of will. We don't need to wait until we have a larger house, more time, or more money to open our homes. We just need to begin with a bigger heart. We need to start now. Even if your children have left the nest there are others who need our time, attention, and our homes. C. S. Lewis wrote, "Indeed, the safest road to hell is the gradual one—the gentle slope, soft underfoot, without sudden turnings, without milestones, without signposts." I believe that this safe road has been taken by many who do not want to sacrifice the time and effort it takes to have open hearts and open homes.

At the battle of Gettysburg, the generals and commanders rallied the troops by simply saying, "Home boys, home!" The prodigal son in Luke 15 was brought back to his senses when he remembered his father's house. We learn in 1 Corinthians 15:24 that Jesus means to deliver His family to the Father. That is exactly what a spiritual woman intends to do; she intends to deliver her family to the Lord, and she intends to influence all those who enter the doors of her home for Christ.

Questions for Discussion

1. Why is it often hard to share our homes with others?

2. How can we make a conscious effort to enlarge our hearts? Will it cost us something?

3. What is the difference between an open heart and an open home and entertaining?

4. Tell about a special occasion when someone you know turned an ordinary meal into an extraordinary relationship?

5. What do you think the author means by asking us to own our homes instead of letting our homes own us?

6. If our families are one working unit to serve the Lord, how can we use our homes to bring others to Christ?

7. How can our homes reflect the New Testament sense of community?

8. What do you think is meant by the term *Christ-esteem?* Do you think that teaching *Christ-esteem* would result in a low self-esteem or a high self-esteem? Why?

Chapter 6

Do You Love Me Enough?

"Do you love me?"

— John 21:14–17 —

In order to understand the kind of love Jesus had for us and the kind of love we should have for other people, we need to look closely at John 21:14–17. Jesus asked Peter three times if he loved Him. The first two times Jesus was actually asking Peter if he "agape" loved him. By using the word *agape,* Jesus was literally asking Peter if he would sacrifice or die for him. The first two times, however, Peter answers that he "phileo" loved Christ. Using this word *phileo,* Peter was telling Jesus that he loved him like a brother. Whether Peter does not understand what Christ is asking of him when Christ uses the word for agape love, or whether Peter is not willing to go so far as to say he will die for Christ, we do not know. We do know that the third time, Jesus asks Peter if he loves him like a brother using the word *phileo* and Peter affirms that he does.

Whether Peter understood it completely or not at that moment, we know that he eventually did die for our Lord. We also need to understand agape love and be willing to live for our Lord. Agape love is love that requires willful sacrifice. The word *agape* in the New Testament refers to a form of love that is more *in motion* than *emotion*. It is the kind of love that Christ has for us. It is the kind of love which says, "I will do what is best for you, even if it costs me something." It means forgiving someone, even when you do not feel like it. It means sharing your home, your time, your talents, and your money with others, even though it may mean more work for you. It means taking a dish or a meal to someone in need, even if this is your day to go shopping.

For a very short time, we tried having Caller ID in our home. It was a nightmare for me. I would see the number come up of an elderly or ill sister whom I knew would need to talk for some time. I would see the number come up of someone who was calling Stan out at night for a hospital visit or for us to come at the death of one of their loved ones. I would see the numbers of young ladies who just needed to talk. I can tell you honestly that many times I considered not answering the phone. And then I began to think about the times that Jesus was interrupted, about the times that He was tired and needed to retreat, but He had compassion on the people who needed Him. Within two weeks I had the Caller ID taken off of our phones. I did not want to become a respecter of persons by having time for whomever I wanted to talk to and neglecting others.

No, I do not like being interrupted by telemarketers anymore than you do, and there are times when I would like to finish a good book, study, or see the end of a program when someone calls. But is that really more important than just being available for someone who needs you?

> *"If you love Me keep My commandments."*
> *—John 14:15*

Agape love says, " I will follow you, Lord, even though it will cost me my precious hours, days, and years."

Agape love is love in motion. It does not rely on emotion in carrying out the will of God. Many important things will not get done in His service if we wait until we feel like doing them. In Matthew 26:39 Christ prayed, "O my Father, if it be possible, let this cup pass from me: nevertheless not as I will, but as thou wilt." Christ did not feel like going to the cross. It sounds as if He may have dreaded the horror that He was about to experience. But He knew it had to be done to fulfill

His Father's will. He knew it had to be done for you and me. In that simple word *nevertheless*, right in the middle of His prayer, we see Christ willfully giving Himself for us.

There will be things that we will not feel like doing; but the spiritually beautiful woman finds great joy in knowing that she will do the Father's will whatever the cost. There was joy set before Christ at the cross. There is great joy set before us if we live our lives manifesting His love to others. Our homes are the perfect place to do that.

We have a son and daughter-in-law who are very good at personal evangelism. They have converted several people to the Lord. Their method makes it look so easy and natural, which I believe it is to them. They befriend people. They spend time with them. They invite people into their home and spend hours with them. The time spent is not always in Bible study. As a matter of fact, much of the time is spent just talking or playing games. Many times they bring the friend to worship and Bible study. The friend begins asking questions and often such contacts become Christians. This is friendship evangelism. It is New Testament Christianity in action. One does not have to preach to win souls for the Lord. We often feel overwhelmed because there may not seem to be time to teach

> *"Let him know that he who turns a sinner from the error of his way will save a soul from death and cover a multitude of sins."*
> *—James 5:20*

everyone; but there is time to focus on one. By befriending someone and sharing your home and your love for the Lord with them, you may save a soul from death.

Let me share with you what can happen when you focus on one precious soul who enters your home. The three boys and I met Steven at Bible camp when he was 13 or 14. He was a stranger to us. Generally we knew most of the children and their parents. Steven had been invited to camp by a sweet Christian young lady and for some reason he had decided to take her up on the offer. During the course of the week, my sons got to know Steven better. Several times that summer after camp, he came to our house, and then more often during the next school year. When he was not with us, I felt like he was hanging with a group that was not really good for him, but he had a love for hunting, and his friends were his hunting buddies. My sons loved hunting, and over the next couple of years, Steven replaced his old friends with our three boys. He spent lots of time at our house. By the time he was 16, he had been suspended from public school for fighting. I was told that he was defending his younger sister. Steven was quiet and pensive at first, and I rarely inquired about his personal life. He rarely offered information.

Steven was always well mannered in our home and was a very bright young man. By the time he was 17 he was spending most of his time at our house. He did tell us by now that his parents were going through a divorce and his world was turning upside down. He was clearly frustrated. He studied with us, prayed with us, and lived with our boys.

The day Kyle was leaving for college, he asked me to let Steven—and three other boys who had been spending the summer with him—keep living at our house. Three of the boys went on to college or got jobs within a short time, but Steven stayed. We studied English and he passed the GED.

A year or so later, we suggested that he go to college. He went to a Christian college where he met a wonderful Christian young lady, and soon I knew that they were already getting serious. I cautioned him about how important it was to build a future if he intended to be a husband one day. I also told him that she needed to know everything about his family. All she had really known personally was our family. When they came home for the weekends, they stayed with us. I told him that I expected him to be truthful with her and to do his best to build a strong Christian life for whomever he would marry. We both cried and I could tell that he was being defensive, but I had to treat him as I would have one of my own children.

The night before his wedding a year ago, he called and asked me to come a little early the next day. I was going to be escorted as honorary mother of the groom. It was one of the sweetest moments of my life. Stan and I are as proud of Steven and his wife today as we are of our own children. We treat them exactly as we do our own children. He is finishing his college education and has served as the youth minister for one of the local congregations.

One of the added benefits I have seen over the years for those who have made the decision to live with open hearts and homes is that the peer pressure which many teenagers feel is not so strongly felt by those whose families unreservedly welcome all into their home and into their hearts. There may be a few of your children's friends with whom you would rather they not associate, but in your home, on your turf, the situation is much more manageable. Make sure they are welcome there. When young people see a genuine love for them and for the Lord, they are going to be more likely to understand and respect your home and your children. It doesn't matter how expensive your furnishings are, how many antiques or collectibles you have, or how big of a house you have. If you are not using your home for the Lord, then it is a hindrance to your service to the Lord and to your spiritual beauty. You need to consider some priority changes in order to live an authentic, spiritually beautiful life.

> *"Lord, when did we see You hungry and feed You, or thirsty, and give You drink?"*
> *—Matthew 25:37*

Jesus is coming to your house and He will come in the form of one of the "least of these" (Matthew 25:40, 45). The sheep in Matthew 25 fed the hungry, quenched the thirsty, welcomed strangers, clothed the needy, cared for the sick, and visited those in prison. The goats bleated out excuses for being socially unconscious. Those of us who think that we can serve only those who are like us are blind and indifferent to the "least of these." What we do for the world we do *for* Jesus, we do *because* of Jesus, and as if others truly *are* Jesus.

A Christian home is one of the most natural environments in which to teach others about the Lord and to show them a truly Christ-centered family. A Christian woman is most comfortable and most comforting in this situation. From a human standpoint, I have to admit that there are times when you pull into your driveway and wish for a few moments that you could come home to an empty house. And then you remind yourself that your home is God's home and all are welcome there. Many times, the apostles thought Jesus should depart from the crowds, but there were times when He knew that people needed Him and He could not forsake them. We should feel the same way about those who enter our homes.

☙☙☙☙☙☙☙

Often when I speak to ladies about this subject, I share with them a list of ten little things that mean a lot when one has an open heart and an open home. I would like to share them with you:

1. Leave the lights on most of the time at night. Always leave the house well lit until the last child is home at night. This lets others know that you are home if they have a need, and it makes your own child feel welcome. It also lets your child know that you are waiting for him/her.
2. Let other children spend the night whenever your child asks. Don't mind if some have to sleep on the floor—they won't mind.
3. Have food.
4. Have something cooking after school. Use a crock pot for meat, soup, or chili, or simply cut and bake cookies. The comfort of coming home to something cooking and smelling great is a blessing many children will never know.
5. Make you own family traditions and include visitors in them.
6. Eat together—whatever—whenever. Sometimes we would meet at Bucky's—our local greasy spoon restaurant—as late as 8:30 P.M. just so we could all eat together after sports practice, mowing yards, or other activities. Studies have shown that children whose families eat at least one meal together daily have a much better chance

of excelling in academics. I used to keep all kinds of good reading material in the boys' bathroom upstairs. Sometimes I would add a Post-It note to an article and write, "Required reading." They would know that in a few days we were going to discuss that article at the dinner table. It made for great conversation and intellectual stimulation. Often their friends would have read it, too.

7. Leave notes in a designated place. Always leave a note and always expect to find a note if someone is not home. I noticed one day that the finish was completely off of the back of the chair on which we taped notes for many years. I still love that chair.

8. Don't act shocked about anything you are told or anything you overhear in your home. Don't tell anything you know unless it is a matter of life or death.

9. If your child is driving age and supposed to be at a certain place, feel free to call and ask him/her to bring home a loaf of bread or a carton of milk. (This will serve a couple of very useful purposes.) Also, do not set a definite curfew, but expect a call from your child sometime during the evening letting you know approximately when he/she will be home. Setting exact time limits is conducive to accidents.

10. If it is time for family devotionals, prayer, or family bonding, include whoever is in your home. It may have a very strong influence on their lives in the future.

In order to live with an open heart and an open home, you may have to lighten up. You may have to loosen your grip. You may learn to laugh more. Make sure that you own your house and that it does not own you. Remember: it is the Lord's house, or they labor in vain that build it anyway.

Questions for Discussion

1. What is agape love? Give examples of it?

2. How did Christ manifest agape love to us? How can we manifest it to others?

3. What is friendship evangelism? Give an example of it from the New Testament. Give an example of someone you know who is good at friendship evangelism and list the character traits that make them good at it. How can we develop some of those traits?

4. Is there a person in your life for whom your home has made a difference? Share the experience with the class. How can you find others with whom you can share your love for the Lord in your home?

5. Why do you think that peer pressure may not be such a strong influence on young people from an open Christian home?

6. How can your home actually be a hindrance to you in serving others for Christ? Are you willing to make your home an asset in your spiritual life? How can you do that?

7. Has Jesus come to your house? Did you recognize Him or did you let the opportunity pass? How can we take advantage of opportunities for serving others in our homes?

Chapter 7

ᘓᕲᘓᕲᘓ

Building Her House

"The wise woman builds her house."
— Proverbs 14:1 —

It saddens me to know that many young ladies do not realize the value or the scriptural directive of homemaking. A few years ago, one of the young men who was living with us brought a girl whom he was dating to our home for dinner. I asked her to set the table. She caustically said, "Okay, I guess I'll do the woman thing."

Just a few days earlier I had read an article extolling the annual "take your daughter to work" day, and I immediately thought that we need a "take your daughter home" day. Many young ladies have no idea what it means to manage a household and to practice hospitality. We have raised a generation of "material girls" who, often through no fault of their own, look forward more to Mondays when they can take their children to day care and go to an office than to Fridays when they can spend precious time with their families. Certainly many young ladies know more about computers than housekeeping.

> *"She watches over the ways of her household."*
> *—Proverbs 31:27*

We have been programmed to believe that we can be superwomen. However, Superwoman exists only either on television, living her life by a script with all of the props, or in our imaginations. We simply cannot be the best at everything at the same time. We cannot be the best employee, the best boss, the best wife, the best parent, the best homemaker, the best Christian, the best friend, and the best employer all at the same time. In every area of our lives we have to make choices. Our choices decide if we have time to influence others by sharing our time and resources with them or if we have a mortgage

"You cannot serve God and mammon."
—Matthew 6:22

so large that husband and wife both have to work just to pay for the house. A materialistic lifestyle may show the world a beautiful house, but it takes a dreadful toll on the home. We need not try to keep up with the Joneses. (Anyway, just when we are about to catch up with them, they refinance.) We do not want our homes ruled by materialism. We want to have time to enjoy our homes, our families, and the lives of others.

Many of the best memories in your life and in the lives of those around you may be the spontaneous ones. You cannot orchestrate the best memories of a lifetime in just a few minutes of quality time. Have you ever had a pumpkin fight with your children? (This is the result of cleaning out the inside of a pumpkin and casually tossing it toward one of your children. It is a memory they will never forget.) How about a Jello fight? Or have you had time to enjoy a grandchild playing in the biscuit dough? Have you ever had an unexpected guest brighten your day? Has anyone ever called and asked you just to pray with her? Have you ever been available for another woman's child who may be hurting?

One of the startling facts I have come to understand in the life of Christ was that He did not carry a Daytimer. The only Palm Organizer He carried was His prayerful hands. He did not use His time in a rush and flurry of activity and keep a record of every task accomplished. He had time for people. He had time to talk to the Samaritan woman at the well. He had time to tell stories. He had time to teach. He had time to heal and tend to the sick. He made time to spend with His Father alone. He had time to hold the children. His life obviously did not consist of the abundance of the things He possessed. Or did it? He certainly possessed the spiritual things. How very different from our world's view of success.

Recently when a young couple had been staying in our home for a few weeks, the young wife asked me if I had a brush for the commode in the downstairs bathroom. I guess I should have had one, but the truth is that I have always used an old rag and disinfectant and cleaned the commodes with my hands. When I told her that, she cringed and said, "You mean you have actually put your hand in the commode?"

I couldn't help but smile and think of all the times over the years while cleaning the bathrooms that I had thanked God for my home, my family, and His bountiful blessings. I thanked Him that I had nice bathrooms to clean and friends who wanted to be in our home. I always looked at that as part of my service to Him.

Now I hope you understand that I am not saying you have to actually put your hand in the commode to be thankful or spiritual, but I am saying that you have to be willing to do whatever job needs to be done without murmuring and complaining with whatever resources you have available with all of your heart to the Lord. If you prefer using a brush, wholeheartedly have at it!

We have forgotten in our "get ahead" culture that the person who serves is the greatest among us. Read the entire chapter of Matthew 25. These people were spiritual. Serving others was a way of life for them. Whether it is in our homes, in the church, or in the world, a spiritual person is found serving others. Christ could have left His apostles many things. He could have left His memoirs for them to sell later and become rich. He could have left them an army. But what did Christ leave His dearest friends as their final gift from Him? We learn in John 13, beginning in verse 5, that He left them a towel. He washed their dirty feet and left them the greatest lesson the world could ever learn. He left them an example of true greatness and humility. I have heard it said that self-pity brings a person down but true humility lifts a person up. Christ was the supreme example of humility and when He was lifted up from the earth, He drew all men unto Him (John 12:32).

After I had finished speaking on this subject at a ladies' day, one of the young ladies got up and made announcements. Then she said, "Well, Ms. Sheila, I think after today that I will not be so uptight if someone comes to visit and my house is not perfect. And I think I could pick someone else's kids up from school in my not-so-clean car. But do I have to wash feet?" I was thankful that she was beginning to get the point. She was just beginning to understand that the spiritually beautiful woman will do whatever needs to be done at the moment for the Lord and for her fellow man without hesitation, without reservation, and joyfully. Spiritual beauty may eventually find this young lady.

> *"If I then, your Lord and Teacher, have washed your feet, you also ought to wash one another's feet."*
> *—John 13:14*

Let me share with you an excerpt from a letter that Stan and I received from a young lady just a few days ago:

> I just want you both to know how grateful I am for the influence you have had on my life. There were several of us who came to Water Valley [the congregation for which Stan was preaching at the time] around the age of 18 and you both did so much for us! You opened up so many avenues for us. You always welcomed us into your home. You made sure we always had good Christian ways to have fun. That was such an important thing to teach us. You have helped us see over the years that we can have fun and laugh with good friends without going to clubs or parties. Now, I am a few years older with a husband of my own, new home, new family members and I just pray that I will use the things you have taught me in classes as well as the way you both live your lives. I just can't tell you both how much you have helped me over the years. Thank you both!
>
> With love, Jenny

I truly believe that Jenny is well on her way to becoming a spiritually beautiful person.

The story is told of a little girl getting off of the school bus with her good friend. Her mother saw her through the window, as she was standing at the kitchen sink, and expected her daughter to come running up the walk in just a few minutes. However, after several minutes her child did not come up the walkway and the mother began to worry. As she was going out the front door, her small daughter came running up the walkway.

"What took you so long, Emma," her mother asked, "I was beginning to get worried about you."

"Well," said her daughter, "Samantha was having a problem and I really had to help her with it."

"How did you help her?" her mother asked.

"I just sat down and helped her cry," said the precious little girl.

Have you ever just sat down and helped someone cry? Is your life so well ordered that you would have time to do that? Do you know how to say "no" to the unimportant things so that you can be available for the important things like helping someone cry?

The spiritually beautiful woman has her priorities in order and lives her life according to those priorities. She has strength and courage enough not to let the world dictate her actions and her way of life. She learns dependence on God by giving her time and talents and literally herself to becoming a glory goal for Him. She does this so that the world will glorify God because of the way she has chosen to live her life. Each one of us has that power within us.

Questions for Discussion

1. In what ways does a wise woman build her house spiritually? Do we often worry more about building it physically? Which will be most lasting?

2. What is the truth about Superwoman?

3. Discuss the virtues of Proverbs 31 and apply them to our lives. Would good nutrition be applicable here? Buying and selling real estate? Being thrifty?

4. Share with the class a precious memory that was created spontaneously in your home?

5. What would be our best Palm Organizer?

6. Ask someone to read John 13:1–17. How can we apply this to our lives every day?

7. Add your suggestions to the ten practical suggestions for keeping your home open and inviting to others. Share your thoughts with the class.

Chapter 8

⊙⊘⊙⊙⊚⊙

In the World, Not of the World

"For you, brethren, have been called to
liberty; only do not use liberty as an opportunity for the flesh, but through love
serve one another."   — Galatians 5:13

What freedom we have in Christ! So many scriptures as-
sure us that our life in Christ is one of great liberty. As Christian women in the twenty-first century, we have more of an
opportunity than ever before to make a difference in the
world—to let our light dispel the darkness.

Over the past 2000 years, sincere Christians have taken
very different views concerning our responsibility to the world.
Some believe we should separate ourselves from the world
and have as little part in it as possible. Certainly Christ did
not do that.

Others believe that we should force our morality on our
culture. Those people would try to make others conform to the
morality of the Scriptures. Even though Christ often taught
the perilous results of not living the Christian life, He would
not make anyone follow Him. I truly believe that if He was
going to make anyone follow Him, it might have been the rich
young ruler. Mark tells us that Jesus loved him (Mark 10:21).
However, Jesus knew that following Him must be a willful choice,
just as His death on the cross had to be willful submission on
His part.

In order for us to see how the early Christians were viewed by the world, let us look at an anonymous letter entitled "Letter to Diognetus" which Dr. M. Norvel Young shares with us in his book *Living Lights, Shining Stars*. This letter possibly dates to the second century.

Those Christians

For Christians are not differentiated from other people by country, language, or customs; you see, they do not live in cities of their own, or speak some strange dialect, or have some peculiar lifestyle.

This teaching of theirs has not been contrived by the invention and speculation of inquisitive men; nor are they propagating mere human teaching as some people do. They live in both Greek and foreign cities, wherever chance has put them. They follow local customs in clothing, food, and other aspects of life. But at the same time, they demonstrate to us the wonderful and certainly unusual form of their own citizenship.

They live in their own native lands, but as aliens; as citizens, they share all things with others; but like aliens, suffer all things. Every foreign country is to them as their native country, and every native land as a foreign country.

They marry and have children just like everyone else; but they do not kill unwanted babies. They offered a shared table, but not a shared bed. They are present "in the flesh," but they don't live "according to the flesh." They are passing their days on earth, but are citizens of Heaven. They obey the appointed laws, and go beyond the laws in their own lives.

They love everyone, but are persecuted by all. They are unknown and condemned; they are put to death and gain life. They are poor and yet make many rich. They are short of everything and, yet, have plenty of all things. They are dishonored and, yet, gain glory through dishonor.

Their names are blackened and, yet, they are cleared. They are mocked and bless in return. They are treated outrageously and behave respectfully to others. When they do good, they are punished as evildoers; when punished, they rejoice as is being given new life. They are attacked by Jews as aliens, and are persecuted by the Greeks; yet those who hate them cannot give any reason for their hostility.

To put it simply—the soul is to the body as Christians are to the world. The soul is spread through all parts of the body and Christians through all the cities of the world. The soul is in the body but it is not of the body; Christians are in the world but not of the world.

One wonders if Christians today would be referred to as the soul of the world? Certainly since the tragic events of September 11, 2001, many want to believe that God is the soul of America, but just because we have "In God We Trust" printed on our currency does not make it so.

In light of so many things, how do we individually decide our responsibility as Christians to the world? If we look at Christ's in-

> *"Whatever your hand finds to do, do it with your might."*
> *—Ecclesiastes 9:10*

volvement in the world, as well as the example of the Good Samaritan that He gave us in Luke 10, we will discover that the Christian woman is to live in the world, in service to her God and her fellow men. We must let God be glorified in us by the things we do for others in this world.

The spiritually minded woman today has no excuse for not knowing what is going on in the world. And she has no excuse for not caring.

The Good Samaritan—who was not by any means "good" to those who were listening to Jesus, but hated by them—provided money, transportation, his own time and energy, and a credit card to someone whom he did not even know. The only thing the Samaritan knew was that the person lying before him was in need. That is all we should need to know.

The Samaritan obviously had respect for life. He had compassion. He had the means of making a difference. The spiritually beautiful woman will take her example of social ethics from him.

Those who promote abortion, homosexuality, pornography, violence, and a host of immoral lifestyles are not passive. Neither can we be. Edmund Burke, an eighteenth-century statesman was correct in saying, "The only thing necessary for the triumph of evil is for good men to do nothing." That was never more true than it is today.

We may have thought for the past 60 years that the Lord would intervene and not let us become so much like Sodom and Gomorrah. We may have thought that our leaders would eventually stand for goodness and righteousness by knowing that righteousness exalts a nation (Proverbs 14:34).

Unfortunately, most of our politicians have very little knowledge of the Word of God, and if they happen to be believers, they would be hard pressed to vote their consciences for fear of losing a broad base of voters. Al Gore, during the 2000 presidential campaign, publicly said that John 16:3 was his favorite Bible verse. That verse says, "And these things they will do to you because they have not known the Father or Me." It is a fitting verse for him to use considering his stance on abortion, homosexuality, and his obvious ignorance of the Scriptures. He was undoubtedly trying to use John 3:16.

No amount of "spin" will make our lives more acceptable to our Lord. As Christian women we are going to be judged by how we walk in this world. On the Day of Judgment there will be no explaining, no covering up, no excuses, no scapegoat, no speeches, no press conferences, no "war rooms," and no second chance to get it right. There will be no amendments and no majority vote. Only one vote will matter.

Consequently, one of the most important things we need to understand as we seek to please our Lord in this world is found in Ecclesiastes 3:11 which tells us that God has set eternity in our hearts. That literally means that until we understand eternity and our relationship to it, we cannot be satisfied. All of those who are searching for some deeper meaning in their lives through the world and its sordid pleasures will never be able to find it. All of those who are searching for genuine happiness by storing up treasures on this earth will never find it. True happiness will elude them. It is not when we have a finer house, a newer car, brilliant children, or a cure for cancer that we will be truly satisfied. We will be truly satisfied only when we understand our destination for eternity, when we realize that we are already living in eternity, and when we understand our relationship to our Creator, our fellow men, and eternity. Then, and only then,

> *"Lay up for yourselves treasures in heaven . . . For where your treasure is, there your heart will be also."*
> *—Matthew 6:20–21*

can we truly understand our relationship to the world and find contentment in it.

Several years ago when we were building a house, I just knew that when we finally got to move into the house, I would be truly happy. But soon after moving in, I began thinking that I needed a new dining room suite for the new house. Shortly after that, I began thinking that I needed new prints for the walls, and not long after that I decided I didn't really like the carpet I had chosen.

You see, until we understand our relationship to eternity, we can never be completely satisfied with material things. There will always be more things to want. I have a friend who is extremely wealthy and I am constantly amazed at the many ways she finds to spend all that money! The purchase of a horse leads to buying a stable . . . a pair of water skis leads to an expensive ski boat and a lake house . . . a desire for a tan leads to a personal tanning bed . . . a bigger car leads to a Hummer . . . you get the point!

The only things that truly matter will be those things we have done for others and those things we have done in service to our Lord in view of eternity. Once we realize that, our dining room suites will probably be sufficient. We will realize that the prints we have will work fine. And if you are like me, you will be satisfied with that carpet for a long time.

The New Testament gives countless examples of Christians who were making the world a better place. It gives examples of Christians who were working to gain wealth in the world, which they, in turn, were using to help others. It gives examples of women keeping house, selling linens, buying real estate, making tents, and a host of other secular activities. The Bible even gives us examples of Christians who were in the government. It is impossible for Christians to live outside this physical world. We can only live in many respects like normal people live.

Thankfully, however, Christ prayed for you and me in John 17,

> I do not pray for these alone, but also for those who will believe in Me through their word; that they all may be one, as You, Father, are in

me, and I in You; that they also may be one in Us, that the world may believe that You sent Me (John 17:20–21).

Earlier in that chapter Christ had prayed,

I do not pray that You should take them out of the world, but that You should keep them from the evil one. They are not of the world, just as I am not of the world. Sanctify them by Your truth. Your word is truth (John 17:15–17).

Christ prayed that we might be able to live *in* the world but not *of* the world and that we would be sanctified by the Word of God, having it written on our hearts and in our minds.

It is ironic to me that God was so often invoked at the inauguration of George W. Bush in January 2001 by a people by whom He must be so often provoked. There was a prayer at the beginning of the ceremony and a prayer at the conclusion, but it is not legal to have a prayer in public schools. Is there something wrong with this picture?

The oath of office was administered, accepted, and sworn to with one hand on the Bible by both the President and the Vice-President. This is our tradition. The minister who had the invocation actually dedicated the inauguration to God. I am reminded of the events of Matthew 15 and Mark 7 when Christ told the Scribes and Pharisees, "Well did Isaiah prophesy of you hypocrites, as it is written: This people honors me with their lips, but their heart is far from me. And in vain they worship me, teaching as doctrines the commandments of men" (Mark 7:6–7).

Our responsibility as Christian women in this world is to make absolutely sure that Isaiah's prophecy does not apply to us. We never want to look like whitewashed tombs to our Lord (Matthew 23:27). "For we shall all stand at the judgment seat of Christ" (Romans 14:10).

A few years ago, I had the privilege of hearing Guy Dowd, National Teacher of the Year in 1986, relate this poignant story. It was his wake-up call in understanding the kind of love Christ had for us. It exemplifies the kind of love we should have for others.

Guy said that he was in college at the time and had been up studying for a final exam all night. He was ravenously hungry. He said he went into the diner nearest the campus and ordered just about everything on the breakfast menu. He said he was starving.

In the meantime an older couple came in off of the street and sat directly across from him. The man had no teeth and a very large nose that seemed to be much more on one side of his face than the other. He said that one of the man's ears was extremely large and he talked loudly and almost unintelligibly. The woman, apparently his wife, had dark brown teeth and hundreds of potmarks all over her face. Her eyes were set way back in her head and crossed. Her hair was dirty and tangled. Guy said that they were grotesque looking. They looked like they had just been let out of a day home for the mentally retarded. He said that he immediately lost his appetite. He knew he could not eat a bite with those two sitting across from him.

Guy was about to get up and leave when a pretty young mother and her beautiful blond four-year-old daughter walked into the diner. He said the little girl was gorgeous. She was the picture of innocence and purity.

All at once, the old woman spied the little girl and cried out to her, "You are so beautiful! Come over here little girl and give me a kiss!"

The little girl looked at her mother who nodded that it was okay.

Guy said that he was furious. He thought, "How can *you*—expect *her*—to kiss *that*?"

The little girl walked over to the woman, cupped the frightfully scarred face into her hands and kissed it.

"Jesus loves you!" she said.

Guy said that he was immediately struck with the realization that God did love that strange couple–just as much as He loved him, the little girl's kind mother, or the beautiful little girl.

When he got back to his room he suddenly noticed, as if for the first time, the poster that was hanging on his dorm room wall. It was the picture of a homeless man in a drunken stupor. The caption read: "You only love the Lord as much as you love the least of these."

He began thinking that compared to God he was much more like the old couple and the drunken man. God's ways are so much higher than our ways and yet He reaches down and loves us unconditionally.

In a society that has begun manufacturing "designer babies," it will be the sincere, dedicated Christians who show the rest of the world how to love society's unlovable.

Questions for Discussion

1. How can we use our spiritual light as Christians to dispel the darkness in the world?

2. Should we physically separate ourselves from the world as Christians? Why?

3. Should we try to force others to follow Christ and His teachings? Why?

4. In what ways can we be like the Good Samaritan?

5. What can we glean from Ecclesiastes 3:11?

6. How can we store up for ourselves treasures in Heaven? Do we take inventory of our lives with this in mind as often as we check our savings account or our retirement funds?

7. Ultimately, how are we as Christians to love the people of the world? (Remember that we talked about agape love being love *in-motion* rather than a love based on *e-motion*.)

8. Jesus touched a leper when it was unlawful to do so. How can we touch the lives of society's unlovable? Is it hard for us to literally give them a hug? Why? Can we overcome our reluctance? How?

Chapter 9

ᘓᓍᕢᘙᘓᕢ

Walking at Liberty

"And I will walk at liberty,
for I seek Your precepts . . ."
— Psalm 119:45 —

True liberation for the spiritually beautiful woman is found in the Word of God. Psalm 119:45–46 tells us that we can "walk at liberty, for I seek Your precepts. I will speak of your testimonies before kings and I will not be ashamed." Also in Mark 8:36–38 we learn,

> For what shall it profit a man if he gains the whole world, and loses his own soul? For what will a man give in exchange for his soul? Or whoever is ashamed of Me and My words in this adulterous and sinful generation, of him the Son of man will also be ashamed when He comes in the glory of His Father with the holy angels.

These verses tell us that we don't have to worry about what the world thinks of us or how much of this world's goods we have been able to accumulate. We are refreshed daily by knowing that we walk at liberty in this world because we seek God's precepts. We are free from the bonds of our fickle culture. We may not be asked to speak of our Lord before kings, but we are asked to speak for Him daily. We may need to speak for Him at a PTO meeting, a city council meeting, a school board meeting, or to our neighbor.

This is not a time in our lives for timidity. We learn in 2 Timothy 1:7 that "God has not given us a spirit of fear, but of power and of love and of a sound mind."

Christian women need to understand their calling in the Lord thoroughly and be able to teach and defend the Word of God and the Christian life. There is an old Chinese proverb that says, "It is better to light one candle than to curse the darkness." Christian women in the world are the candles by which our Lord dispels the darkness.

> *"Strength and honor are her clothing; she shall rejoice in time to come."*
> *—Proverbs 31:25*

It is easy to understand why the Feminist Movement has been so powerful during the last 50 years. At different times, and throughout the world, women have been—and in many cultures still are—degraded, mistreated, and considered second-class citizens. These cultures do not respect the biblical directives to men concerning women. For the most part, they are oppressive in nature.

The esteemed philosopher Schopenhauer pronounced that woman

> is in every respect backward, lacking in reason and reflection . . . a kind of middle step between the child and the man, who is the true human being . . . In the last resort women exist solely for the propagation of the race.

Aristotle stated that women never suffered from baldness because they never used the contents of their heads, and Kant wrote that the "fairer sex" was incapable of reason. In 1770, Parliament passed a law stating that

> any woman, regardless of rank or marital status, who managed to ensnare a husband by the use of perfume, make-up, high heels, girdles, false hair, false teeth, et cetera, would be charged with witchcraft. Her marriage would be pronounced null and void.

A similar law decreed that a woman who gave birth to a stillborn child had better have witnesses to that effect—or she would be charged with infanticide.

In many cultures, a woman's very survival hinged upon finding a husband. Rousseau held that women "ought to learn betimes even to suffer injustice, and to bear insults of a husband without complaint."

Obviously, women have not always been treated fairly and with respect. No one doubts that. However, many of the results of feminism are absurdity as evidenced in a *U.S. News and World Report* article dated August 21, 2000. It is entitled, "Now Sit, Ingvar, Sit."

> Young women in Sweden, Germany, and Australia have a new cause: they want men to sit down while urinating. This demand comes partly from concerns about hygiene—avoiding the splash factor—but, as Jasper Gerard reports in the British *Spectator*, "more crucially because a man standing up to urinate is deemed to be triumphing in his masculinity, and by extension, degrading women." One argument is that if women can't do it, then men shouldn't either. Another is that standing upright while relieving oneself is a "nasty macho gesture," suggestive of male violence. A feminist group at Stockholm University is campaigning to ban all urinals from campus, and one Swedish elementary school has already removed them. Yola, a 25-year-old Swedish trainee psychiatrist, says she dumps boyfriends who insist on standing. "What else can I do?" said her new boyfriend, Ingvar, who sits.

A spiritually beautiful woman will have a clear understanding of male and female roles as God would have them. A scholarly book by John Piper and Wayne Grudem entitled *Recovering Biblical Manhood and Womanhood* would be very helpful to you in understanding God's pattern for the home and for the church. Also, a book by Don McWhorter, entitled *God's Woman: Feminine or Feminist?* is a great read for the woman who is truly concerned about her spirituality and her relationships according to the Scriptures.

> *"As for My people, children are their oppressors, and women rule over them . . . Those who lead you cause you to err, and destroy the way of your paths."* —*Isaiah 3:12*

The word *submission* is not politically correct in this culture. However, Paul realized the power of submission. Christ realized the power of submission. And the spiritually beautiful woman will realize the power of willful submission.

The beatitudes found in the *Sermon on the Mount* in Matthew 5 were not politically correct for that culture either.

Certainly the "poor in spirit," the "meek," or "those who mourn" were not considered successful people. Those attributes certainly did not describe the self-serving scribes and Pharisees. Jesus' teaching was a challenge to the cultural norms of that day just as His teaching is today. It is imperative that we remember, however, that cultures change. The teaching of our Lord and Savior does not.

I am personally convinced that much of the violence in our schools and in our society today is perpetrated by young males who are socially and emotionally confused about their manhood. In college I wrote a lengthy report entitled "The Essence of Gender" based on Hemingway's novel, *The Sun Also Rises*. I am as convinced now as I was then that manhood is more than a body part. Unfortunately, one of the results of militant feminism is that the men in our society are being emotionally and socially emasculated by our culture. Consequently, we are paying a very high price as many of them try to prove their manhood. Just this past year a 15-year-old junior high school student in Santee, California, opened fire on his classmates and smiled as he pulled the trigger, killing two and wounding 13 others. It has been widely reported that he was often ridiculed and never stood up for himself. This time he showed them that he was a man!

I believe that psychologically many young men, as well as middle-aged men, have been emasculated by our society and have no sense of true biblical manhood. There is no rite of passage except violence. This is something that must be addressed in our culture or we will have countless other senseless murders.

The attitudes and actions of the women in a given society play such a very important part in how men feel about themselves in that culture. Men need and want our attention and our affirmation. I read a quip in *Reader's Digest* a few years ago which said that psychologists believed that if women only made love to men who walked on their hands, that within six months 45 percent of the world's population would be walking upside down.

Women have tremendous influence on men. Let's not forget that God gave us that influence. Throughout the Old and the New Testaments, God warns men to stay away from women who would use their influence for evil. The spiritually beautiful woman, the woman after God's own heart, uses her influence to give strength, honor, and dignity to her husband and to those whom she loves.

> *"I press toward the goal for the prize of the upward call of God in Christ Jesus."*
> —*Philippians 3:14*

I wonder if you realize how much of what the men in your life think about themselves is often what they see reflected in your face when they look at you. What does your husband see? Is it disgust? Is it flippancy? Is it knowing that you think there is only one adult at your house and it is you? Or is it admiration?

What does your son think you see in him? A stupid boy? An inept young man? Or a strong young person on his way to becoming a man of God?

What do the men of your congregation see about themselves when they look at you? Do they see disdain? Do they see impatience? Or do they see respect?

On the day that Stan Jr. got married he presented this poem to his dad:

> The question was asked,
> What do you want most in life?
> Fortune, fame, a beautiful wife?
>
> I thought of how wonderful all of that would be,
> But all I really want is for my son to see me,
> As the man I saw my dad to be!

I hope you realize that much of what your children see their father to be comes from you. Do not ever forget that. Do you speak of him with honor and respect? Do you say, "Daddy says we have to do it, so we will." I encourage you with all of the encouragement within me to be the help meet to your husband that you were created to be and that God wants you to be. God instructs men to love their wives enough to die for them and women to love their husbands enough to live for them.

We are told in the Scriptures to press toward the goal in order to win the prize. In the context here, Paul is talking about the prize of eternal life. I strongly believe, however, that we can also win the prize in our marriages, in our homes, and in our congregations if we are willing to be politically incorrect and spiritually beautiful.

Womanhood in its truest sense is the perfect help meet and complement to manhood. In this complete union is God's pattern for the home, the church and the nation. When the pattern is soiled or torn, the strength of the union will be compromised.

One timeless contrast to the feminists' view of womanhood is a woman who changed the course of history by following a man's advice at the risk of her life. Esther was the queen. She was in a position of honor and authority. She could have felt that she had earned everything herself and that she had a right to make her own decisions. She could easily have forgotten about her people and the advice of her guardian. Instead, we see Esther giving us an enduring example of selfless service. After the advice and encouragement of her kinsman Mordecai, she resolved to interfere with a dangerous threat to the Jews, even at the cost of her own life. She told Mordecai:

> *"And the Lord God said, 'It is not good that man should be alone; I will make him a helper comparable to him.'"*
> *—Genesis 2:18*

> Go, gather together all the Jews that are present in Shushan, and fast for me; neither eat nor drink for three days, night or day. My maids and I will fast likewise. And so I will go to the king, which is against the law; and if I perish, I perish!

Here was a woman who had everything for which to live, but she trusted Mordecai and allowed him to advise her to serve the people of God. She did not dismiss his advice or think that she could devise a better plan. She was not ashamed of listening to the instructions of one who was older and wiser than she. I wonder if we are allowing God to use us in this way, or are we constantly afraid of what it may look like in the eyes of the world for us to actually listen to the godly men in our lives?

It is true that shame is humiliating and that women have had to bear shame because of ignorance at various times, in various cultures. However, true humility is a different thing altogether! It is a choice that the spiritually beautiful woman makes because of her strength of character.

Another example of a spiritually beautiful woman who was a light in a world of darkness was Dorcas. Her spiritual beauty was evident by the tears of the widows who stood weeping at her death. She had great influence over the lives of others because of her goodness. She was described as being "full of good works and charitable deeds." She did not need a women's liberation movement to make her feel like somebody. She knew what she was and who she was. She was a servant and because of that attitude of heart she was truly loved. Her beauty, honor and strength were found in serving others. I have heard people say that each of us cried when we were brought into this world and other people rejoiced. We should die in such a way that other people cry when we leave this world, but we will rejoice!

> *"Give her the fruit of her hands, and let her own works praise her in the gates."*
> *—Proverbs 31:31*

Christ came as the light of the world because He knew who He was and His role in view of eternity. Spiritual women will dispel the darkness because they belong to the light, they live in the light, and they are the light. Spiritually beautiful women have eternity set in their hearts and are not ruled by the culture of the day!

Questions for Discussion

1. What does Psalm 119:45–46 mean to us a Christian women? Compare this verse with Matthew 10:32–33.

2. Why do you suppose the author described our culture as "fickle"? Is the Word of God fickle? Share Scriptures with the class on which you based your answer.

3. What is found in 2 Timothy 1:7 that can be of great encouragement to us on our lifetime journey to spiritual beauty?

4. Explain the old Chinese proverb, "It is better to light a candle than to curse the darkness." How can each of us light a candle. Can we dispel the darkness this way?

5. Feminism has resulted from what kinds of cultural attitudes towards women? Contrast these attitudes with Proverbs 31:10–11? What is the difference between demanding respect and commanding respect?

6. In what ways can we pattern our lives after Esther and Dorcas? Why would we want to do that? Will it necessarily be a popular choice?

7. With all honesty and candidness, what do the men in your life see about themselves when they look at you? How can you encourage and strengthen them more with the great influence God has entrusted to you?

8. How can we show the world that we have eternity set in our hearts?

Chapter 10

Real Life and Godliness

> " . . . As His divine power has given to us
> all things that pertain to life and godli-
> ness." — 2 Peter 1:3

If you and two of your friends were having a discussion about the length of a table, one of them might say it is about five feet long. The other one may decide that she thinks the table is about five-and-one-half feet long and you may really believe that the table is not even five feet long. You could discuss it and maybe disagree about it for hours. That is, you could disagree until you take out the tape measure and measure it. When you actually get out the standard and measure the table to be five-and-one-half feet long, the argument ends.

So it is with our values as Christian women in the world. The spiritually beautiful woman will have no doubt that the Bible is the inspired Word of God. She will live her life by that standard. Our values, our lifestyle, and our role in the world are determined by that standard. When we know and understand that standard, we can walk at liberty in the world.

Ours is a secular humanistic society searching for standards today because it has none. If a judge who often tells lies himself is sitting on the bench, how can he prosecute a perjurer? If a judge is a practicing lesbian, how can she condemn immorality? If we accept and condone every lifestyle and sexual preference, who will be able to say what is right? What about bestiality? Incest? Rape? If we are not going to use the Bible for the standard, then our society will continue groping for a consistent measure of right and wrong and there will be none.

Being a spiritually minded woman in such a time as this is a great challenge. As a product of emerging feminism, I grew up believing that I had to secure a wonderful job, make lots of money, have a beautiful house, achieve some notoriety, and dedicate my life to some vocation to be successful. I have since learned that I am valuable, wonderful, successful, and beautiful simply because I am created in the image of God. That understanding liberates the soul of a woman to live authentically and contentedly in the Lord.

We have the greatest power in the world through the knowledge of our self-worth in Christ. We have the greatest advice in the world through the Scriptures. We have more control of our lives than anyone who believes that this world is all there is.

Most people in times of trouble and distress are compelled to stand up and do something. However, the Bible tells us in Exodus 14:13–14 that sometimes we need to just stand down and do nothing. The Lord will fight for us. We can go to a private place, get on our knees, and take advantage of His power. We can be consistent in prayer, going boldly before our Father, asking Him to help us right the wrongs in this world to His glory.

> *"Let me be weighed on honest scales, that God may know my integrity."* —Job 31:6

Another area of our lives in which we can walk at liberty, if we have a secular job, is at our work place. We don't need to leave our integrity, our honesty, or our goodness outside the office door. We need to be exactly who we are on Sunday, on Monday, and every other day of the week. Our employers need to know that we are honest, loyal, have a strong work ethic, and will do everything in our power to be helpful.

Let me hasten to say that spiritual women make excellent employees because they are living out that spirituality every day of their lives. When I worked only three days a week, I realized there were times when I came in on Wednesday that I had been blamed for something that was not my fault. There were also times when I had made mistakes and I readily admitted it. A spiritually beautiful person does not try to make others look bad in order to make herself look better. She does not maliciously talk about others. She goes about her business and makes a point of staying out of anyone else's business unless she can be discreetly helpful. When I decided to quit my part-time job, I received a note from the office manager which read, "Your goodness in this office will be hard to replace." I share this with you only to let you know that goodness is not on your resume but it may be your greatest asset.

A spiritually beautiful woman prays for her employer, her fellow employees, and her work. She includes the Lord in every aspect of her life, and the people who really know her understand that. She reaches out to people who have physical needs as well as spiritual needs. Her co-workers know that she can be trusted to keep a confidence. Let me repeat that: her co-workers know that she can be trusted to keep a confidence! This is extremely important because if you say you will keep a confidence and you do not, you have lied and no one will believe that you are any different from any other employee. This is not only true in the workplace but in every relationship of which you are a part. One of the greatest ways to express your spirituality is to learn to keep quiet. God gave us two ears and one mouth. There is probably a very good reason for that. A spiritually beautiful woman attributes her success in the workplace to the blessing from the Lord that it really is and she continually thanks Him for it.

As Christian women we also need to reach out to the policymakers in our country. If we are commanded to pray for our secular leaders (1 Timothy 2:1–2), then surely we will take advantage of our privilege of voting for them. If you decide not to vote, then you have no right to voice your opinion on how our leaders are handling any given situation.

We need to contact our Senators and Representatives about issues that are coming up for a vote. We need to let them know how we stand. We have been silent for too long—sometimes out of ignorance, sometimes because of apathy. Let's not be guilty of either one.

Let me share with you an excerpt from an article written by John Gallagher in *The Advocate*, the national gay and lesbian news magazine, that appeared before one of our congressional elections:

> The widely anticipated Republican sweep in November's congressional and gubernatorial elections could blunt attempts to advance gay rights and AIDS causes for the next two years, insiders warned. Increased Republican strength is bad news for us, said openly gay Representative Barney Frank (D-Mass). Even as Republicans have softened some on abortion, they have turned up the heat on gay rights.

We really *are* citizens of two worlds while we sojourn on this earth, and consequently we need to make it the best place it can be for teaching others about the Lord and eternity. We need to make it a place where our children and our grandchildren can lead healthful, wholesome physical lives.

I would like to share something with you that came across my desk. This particular article is an indictment of our shallow response to secular humanism. The author was not given. Please read it thoughtfully:

> I Think It Started When . . .
>
> Let's see, I think it started when Madeline Murray O'Hare complained she didn't want any prayer in our schools . . . and in 1963 we said O.K.
>
> Then, someone said you better not read the Bible in school: The Bible that says, "Thou shalt not kill, thou shalt not steal, and love your neighbor as yourself." And we said O.K.
>
> Dr. Benjamin Spock said we shouldn't spank our children when they misbehave because their little personalities would be warped and we might damage their self-esteem. And we said an expert should know what he's talking about, so we won't spank them anymore.
>
> Then someone said teachers and principals better not discipline our children when they misbehave. And the school administrators said no faculty member in this school better touch a student when they misbehave because we don't want any bad publicity, and we surely don't need to be sued . . . And we accepted their reasoning.
>
> Then someone said, "Let's let our daughters have abortions if they want, and they don't even have to tell their parents" . . . And we said that was a good idea.

Then some wise school board member said, "Since boys will be boys and they are going to do it anyway, let's give our sons all the condoms they want so they can have all the fun they desire and we won't have to tell their parents they got them at school" . . . And we said that was a great idea.

Then some of our top elected officials said it doesn't matter what we do in private as long as we do our jobs. And we said it really doesn't matter what anybody, including our President, does in private as long as we have jobs and the economy is good.

And then someone said, "Let's print magazines with pictures of nude women and call it wholesome appreciation for the beauty of the female body." And we said . . . "We have no problem with that."

And someone else took that appreciation a step further and published pictures of nude children and then stepped further by making them available on the internet. And we said . . . "Everyone's entitled to free speech."

And the entertainment industry said, "Let's make T.V. shows and movies that promote profanity, violence, and illicit sex . . . and let's record music that encourages rape, drugs, murder, suicide, and satanic themes" . . . And we said, "It's just entertainment and it has no adverse effect and nobody takes it seriously anyway, so go right ahead."

Now we are asking ourselves why our children have no conscience, why they don't know right from wrong, and why it doesn't bother them to kill strangers, classmates, or even themselves.

☙ ❧ ☙ ❧ ☙ ❧ ❧ ❧ ❧

We are experiencing the bitter fruits of pervasive apathy toward goodness and consistent militancy promoting evil in our society today. In Matthew 5:13 we learn that Christians are to be the salt of the earth. However, we are warned that if we lose our savor we are not worth anything to the Lord. If salt loses its taste, it is worthless. Why would a person even take the trouble to use it? Also, salt has historically been used for preservation. Thankfully, we have refrigerators now but there was a time when meat had to be salted in order to preserve it. If the meat was not salted it began to rot and smell. Even when kept in the basement, unsalted meat would even-

> *"You are the salt of the earth; but if the salt loses its flavor, how shall it be seasoned? It is then good for nothing but to be thrown out and trampled underfoot by men."*
> *—Matthew 5:13*

tually fill the entire house with a terrible odor. Have we as Christians lost our sweet smelling savor and our ability to preserve spiritual goodness? It is very possible that our Lord smells a terrible stench in our nation because we have lost our effectiveness.

It is interesting to note here that William J. Murray, the son of Madeline Murray O'Hare, wrote a book in 1995 entitled *Let Us Pray*. It is, in essence, a brief history of the rise of secular humanism in our culture and a plea for prayer in our schools. He states,

> Many public schools have adopted a version of "secular neutrality" that closely resembles the Supreme Court's. Like the Court's version, schools must recognize secular neutrality for what it is—a distinct, identifiable value system. School prayer, which represents a sacred and moral worldview, has been pushed aside and replaced by an aggressively secular ideology. If we can admit this as a nation and explode the myth of neutrality, we will open up space for competing values, including religion. There is good reason to introduce the sacred back in to schools. Given the current diagnosis of our nation's educational system, is it wise to continue our policy of banning the sacred from schools?

Granted that school prayer is not a panacea for all of the country's social ills, but the lack of all that is religious in our public schools is a symptom of our national disease.

We cannot teach character in schools because we have no standard by which to teach it. I have a friend who teaches first grade. She mentioned the other day how hard it is to teach a young child who does not have a pencil why he cannot steal one from another child who has five or six pencils. She says that of course you should teach him not to steal but try telling him why? Why can't he steal the other child's pencil? He has so many.

Without the Bible there is this huge, oblivious, undefined space called values. It is the equivalent of an endless black hole. We begin asking whose values we are going to teach and why? Then the cycle of cafeteria-style ideology begins. Consequently, there is neither character nor are there any values being taught in public schools except those accepted and instituted by the National Education Association (NEA), of whom Christians should be extremely wary.

Politicians are very unlikely to oppose NEA positions because it may be the single largest fund contributor. You need to know that the NEA is extremely interested in teaching your children sex education. It has instituted many school-based clinics with contraceptive services and abortion referrals in our public schools. The NEA is militant about acceptance and even participation in the homosexual lifestyle. It strongly supports the hiring of homosexual teachers. In order to understand the secular humanism, which the NEA would impose on society through the education of our children, you may want to order a copy of the NEA handbook by sending 10 dollars to NEA Professional Library, P.O. Box 509, West Haven, CT 06516. Read this publication carefully, thoughtfully, and prayerfully to glean the truth about what the NEA would have our children grow up believing, practicing, and teaching.

Christian women especially need to know what is being taught to their children. When our children were in public schools, I found the best way for me to know what was going on in their lives at school was to volunteer for library work, be active in the PTO, and even substitute teach. I made myself available to the teachers and befriended them by working in the classroom

> *"Wisdom has built her house, she has hewn out her seven pillars."*
> *—Proverbs 9:1*

whenever possible. By the end of every school year, I knew which teacher I wanted our children to have the following year and discreetly requested those teachers through the principal. Maybe it was because I had been so supportive that my requests were always granted. All three of the boys had the same teachers for their first four years in public school.

Later, when I taught in a large consolidated high school and noted the apathy of many teachers, parents, and students (in that order), I knew that we needed to find another alternative for our children. Two of them graduated from a Christian school and one of them from a small rural high school. Even those decisions had to be based on the personality and spiritual maturity of each child.

I do believe at this point in time that home schooling is a very viable alternative to the public school system. So many wonderful strides have been made in resources. However, I would caution that every woman does not have the necessary qualities for this extensive endeavor and need not feel guilty if she doesn't. It takes an extremely disciplined and dedicated person whose children know that she is in control at all times to be able to educate her children successfully to their greatest potential. It is a decision that must be prayerfully considered and not embarked upon lightly.

The wise woman will know what goes on in the schools her children are attending and she will be a part of the work going on there. Because we are walking at liberty we will not let our children or our grandchildren be indoctrinated by the mandates of the NEA in a secular humanistic society.

The spiritually beautiful woman in the world understands that if she is ashamed of the Word of God in this adulterous and sinful generation, her Lord will be ashamed of her when He comes in the glory of His Father with the holy angels (Mark 8:38). She understands her responsibility as a temporary citizen of this world and as a citizen of the next world. Her true liberty rests in living daily with that understanding. She is joyous in her freedom by trying to do something every day reflecting the love of Christ while she rests in the knowledge that her eternal "citizenship is in heaven, from which we also eagerly wait for the Savior, the Lord Jesus Christ" (Philippians 3:20).

Questions for Discussion

1. As women who are seeking spiritual beauty, what should be our standard in every aspect of our daily lives? Why?

2. What is meant by the term *secular humanism?* You may ask someone in class to give a brief overview of this belief that has become the religion of our culture.

3. Why is it important that we maintain our integrity as Christians in our workplace? Is it harder to do there than when we are with other Christians? Why? Would the Lord be pleased with your attitude and effort at your workplace? Are you?

4. Why is it important to be trusted to keep a confidence? (See Ecclesiastes 10:20 and Proverbs 11:9.)

5. What is a sojourner? How are we, as Christian women, citizens of two worlds?

6. What does the essay "I Think It Started When" reveal about our culture? How can apathy or militancy destroy a nation?

7. If we are emulating Christ, will we be apathetic? (See Matthew 23:13–16; 21:12; and Mark 11:15–17.)

Chapter 11

⟡⟡⟡⟡⟡

Seeking Spiritual Beauty in the Church

"For as the heavens are higher than the earth, so are my ways higher than your ways, and my thoughts than your thoughts." — Isaiah 55:9

"Do you mean that if a Christian man walked into this gathering of women right now, you would sit down and either he would lead the class or we would have to continue at another time?" the young woman asked me incredulously.

"Yes," I answered. "because I understand from 1 Timothy, chapter 2, verse 12 that I am not to exercise authority over a man in teaching spiritual things," I answered.

"Even though you may be more qualified to teach and better able to communicate God's Word on this subject?" she snapped back accusingly.

"Certainly," I answered. "God's order for His church in this world is not based on my qualifications or my speaking ability." I continued, "If we want to know why women are not to exercise authority over men in the body of Christ we need only to continue our reading of 1 Timothy, chapter 2. The Bible gives us explicitly two reasons that women are not to exercise authority over men in the church. In verses 13 and 14 we are told, "For Adam was first formed, then Eve. And Adam was not deceived, but the woman being deceived, fell into transgression."

Apparently the young woman doing the questioning was a doctor who was attending the ladies' retreat at which I was speaking. I went on to ask her if she had ever been employed by someone and known that she was smarter than her boss and could do the job better than her boss.

"Of course," she answered.

"But did that make you the boss?" I asked her.

Whether we like it or not, the biblical directives given to women in the church cannot be changed for culture or for personal preference. The two reasons given here are entirely separate from the cultures of the first century or the twenty-first century. Neither the creation order nor the fact that Eve was deceived changes because of the customs or the culture in which you live.

> *"There is a way that seems right to a man, but its end is the way of death." —Proverbs 16:25*

Any one of us recognizes that there must be order in place for the accomplishment of goals. As we have mentioned throughout this book about many other aspects of our spiritual lives, the church, too, is a glory goal for God. God will only be glorified through the church by each one of us doing her best individually to serve in the roles that God has given us.

The church is not run by a board of directors. Contrary to what many people think, God does not need our vote, nor does He need to ask us if we think the organism of the church is put together properly or needs to be redesigned. Notice that I said the *organism* of the church and not the *organization*. The church is consistently referred to as a body—a living organism—in the New Testament and the spiritually beautiful woman understands that she is a vital part of that viable organism.

My good friend had not been feeling well for a couple of weeks. She looked perfectly beautiful on the outside. You would think that she was the picture of health. But she had been tired lately. She went to her physician who did a myriad of tests and realized that her internal organs were full of cancer. He believed that the cancer started in the ovaries and then spread to the liver and other places. He told her that 85 percent of her liver had been destroyed. Now you tell me: is that liver a vital and extremely important part of her body? Of course it is. Can we live without our liver? No. But do you see it every day? Is it an obvious part of the body? Is it a part of the body that is very attractive or gets much attention? Hardly! It is, however, a part of the body that is essential to the life of the body.

The spiritually beautiful woman places a high priority on, and is committed to, the body of Christ. She loves and respects that body of which she is a part. For her to talk badly about the other members of that body or try to hurt any part of that body would, in turn, hurt her very much. If you cut your finger slicing a tomato, the red blood cells, the white blood cells, your brain waves, and every other part of your body empathize and try to help. Your brain, the rest of the fingers, and your hand don't try to open that cut and in so doing hurt it more. They don't decide to cut it off. Instead, other body parts instantly begin doing everything in their power to help. Your body is created that way. So should it be with the members of the body of Christ.

The world will not help us understand our responsibilities in the spiritual kingdom. Many books have been written trying to explain, expound upon, or redirect God's plan for women in the church. Many times the books that have been written, which could have been helpful to us, were written by men who were insensitive to the needs and reactions of women, and consequently have caused many women to rebel or, as is more common in the church, simply to do nothing. I sincerely believe that this is why it is imperative for the older women in the church to be teaching younger women as we have been commanded to do.

It is essential that the spiritually beautiful woman understands, willfully accepts, and rejoices in her responsibilities in the Lord's body. She is uniquely qualified to serve in her God-given capacity! Is she to lead? *Emphatically yes*—in her designated areas of the body. We know that she is to manage her household well, to train her children, to teach by example, to sing, and to teach younger women. But is she to lead Christian

men in the work and worship of the body? *Emphatically no*—
that is the men's designated work in the body. Just as the heart
would not be effective trying to do the work of the liver, each of
us is most effective in our God-given roles.

One wonders if Satan did not hate Adam and Eve from the
beginning. Satan was certainly never going to see Heaven
again; he certainly did not want Adam and Eve to, either. Adam
and Eve had paradise; he had torment. They had God; he had
total alienation from God. They had Heaven; Satan could never
go there again. Satan was very anxious for the man or woman
to sin. The Bible tells us that Eve saw that the fruit was good.
That implies that the serpent actually tasted the fruit in front
of her and obviously *he* didn't die. What she did not realize was
that he was already dead—eternally separated from God. And
that is exactly what Satan wants every one of us to be.

It is worthwhile to note in Genesis 3 that we have no account of Eve's discussing her choice with Adam. She seems to
have taken the initiative in this spiritual matter. I have often
pondered how our destinies might have been different had Eve
first sought Adam's advice. Or what if she had had a godly
mother to consult, or even an older woman who loved God and
walked in His ways? Eve, however, took it upon herself to make
the decision to disobey God. We read of God's asking her in Genesis 3:13, "What is this you have you done?"

Do you think that God did not know what she had done? Of
course He did. What God was asking Eve was if *she* really understood what she had done and if she comprehended the im-
plication of her actions for eternity.

God created a very powerful being when He created woman.
The story is told of a five-year-old boy in the hospital with third-
degree burns on 85 percent of his body. He lay there for hours
pathetically crying, "Mommy, Mommy, I want my Mommy," even
though he knew that his own mother had doused him with
kerosene and lit him with a match! Above every person in the
world, he still wanted his mommy. God created women as powerful and influential creatures!

We all know of men who have given up their homes, families, children, and careers for the love of a woman. Certainly

Samson did. And David, a man after God's own heart, took another man's wife and had her husband killed. Adam, the Bible tells us, was not deceived but ate of the forbidden fruit anyway because of the influence of his wife.

Make no mistake about it, God's directives to women to be quiet, to be submissive (1 Timothy 2:11), to be silent in the assembly (1 Corinthians 14:34) are not due to her lack of gifts, intellect, or influence. It is merely one of the ways in which the body of Christ will bring glory to the Father on this earth and the world will see that we are different out of our love and obedience to our Lord. It is another of His ways that is so much higher than our ways. Women's role in the body is not politically correct in the year 2004 but it *is* spiritually beautiful for eternity!

I heard a preacher say recently that God's directives to women have always been hard for us to keep and that is why Paul had to address them several times in the New Testament.

My admonition to you, as you sincerely try to be what God wants you to be, is to read and study the passages that deal with your responsibilities in the body of Christ for yourself. Look at 1 Corinthians 11; 1 Corinthians 14; Ephesians 5; 1 Timothy 2. Listen to what God is saying in these verses. The truth lies within them and not anywhere else.

There have been many attempts by writers and scholars to make Galatians 3:27–28 applicable to the responsibilities of women in the body and teach that men and women have the same responsibilities in the body. A careful reading of this passage, however, in its context, is telling each of us that we have equal access to God in Christ; that we all have the same Father and the same inheritance because of that relationship.

Beginning in verse 24,

Therefore the law was our tutor to bring us to Christ, that we might be justified by faith. But after faith has come, we are no longer under a tutor. For you are all sons of God through faith in Christ Jesus. For as many of you as were baptized into Christ have put on Christ. There is neither Jew nor Greek, there is neither slave nor free, there is neither male nor female, for you are all one in Christ Jesus. And if you are Christ's, then you are Abraham's seed, and heirs according to the promise.

It sounds like we are all just one family doesn't it?

There were five children in my family growing up, girls and boys, and we were all Kecklers. However, we all had different responsibilities. We did not have a dishwasher and my older brother had the job of washing the dishes. However, I always wanted to be the dishwasher. But because he was the oldest, he got to be the dishwasher and I had to dry the dishes. I hated that responsibility mainly because I could not get my work done until he decided to wash. Sometimes he would wait until an hour after supper!

The passage in Galatians 3 says nothing about our responsibilities in the Lord. It does tell us that we are all equal heirs of our Father with equal access to Him regardless of our physical backgrounds. We should rejoice in the fact that it makes us all a part of the body of Christ by being heirs according to the promise. Those who have chosen to use this verse to justify the public roles of women in the body have taken it out of context and tried to make the verse say something that it does not say.

We spoke earlier in this book about coming to the Word of God with a pure heart. The person with a pure heart wants to know what God is saying to us—not what we want Him to say or what the world tells us that He is saying. We must study the Scriptures for ourselves as unencumbered as we can be from our own preconceived ideas, our traditions, and our own desires. However, I don't believe that we need "to be so open minded," as one man penned, "that our brains have fallen out."

We live in a culture that gives great credence to our emotions. That mindset, however, is a dangerous path to follow because our emotions change from day to day. We cannot and must not depend on our emotions to guide us, as Christian women, on our journey to seeking spiritual beauty. The spiritually beautiful woman will be seeking to please her Lord as she carries out her responsibilities in the body of Christ. She will have no other motive.

The New Testament is full of examples of women laboring in the gospel by helping, either financially or with hospitality, those who preach. Lydia, after being baptized, entreated Paul and Silas and Timothy to come to her house and stay (Acts 16:15). A woman can share the gospel with those who are not Christians

> *"If you have judged me faithful to the Lord, come to my house and stay."* —Acts 16:15

and demonstrate Christ in her own life by the way she lives. A woman can sing, pray, and teach other women and children spiritual things. As a matter of fact, in Titus 2:3–5 the older women are commanded to teach the younger women.

After many years of being in the body of Christ, I understand why God instructed the older women to teach the younger. There are some biblical principles that are easier to accept and understand by younger women when they are taught by an older, spiritually beautiful woman. The younger women will see the strength, beauty, confidence in Christ, and contentment that comes from the knowledge and experience the older woman has gleaned from living her life unreservedly for Christ. A spiritually beautiful woman teaching a class of younger women to love the Lord, to love their husbands, to love their children, and to manage their households well is one of the richest blessings in Christ for everyone involved. God knew that.

Questions for Discussion

1. What two reasons are given in 1 Timothy 2 for men to take the public lead in the body of Christ? Are either one of these reasons changed by the culture in which we live?

2. What is meant by the church being a "glory goal" for God in this world?

3. Why is the church described as an organism throughout the New Testament? Could regeneration be involved here? Defend your answer.

4. Is it easier for us to understand our importance in the body of Christ when we see our responsibilities in relationship to the organism of the church rather than the organization of the church? Why?

5. In the organism of the body (the church) are we each dependent on the other? Is our visibility in the world all that important? Why or why not?

6. Why do we sometimes think it is necessary for the world to see our importance? Is there a difference in the spiritually beautiful woman and the women of the world in this respect? In what way?

7. Why is it important for each of us, as women who want to become beautiful in God's sight, to read and study the Word for ourselves? Why isn't the world going to direct us to Christ?

8. Why can't we take everything that is being preached on women's role in the church as the truth? Why should we be more like the Bereans in Acts 17:11–12?

Chapter 12

⌒⌒⌒⌒⌒

After God's Own Heart

"The Lord has sought for Himself
a man after His own heart."
— 1 Samuel 13:14—

Samuel had been told by God to go to Bethlehem to anoint the future king of Israel. How proud Jesse must have been when he brought his sons before Samuel! He may have been especially proud of his oldest son Eliab, because when Eliab was brought before him, Samuel exclaimed, "Surely the Lord's anointed is before Him!" (1 Samuel 16:6). Eliab must have been tall, dark, and handsome. He was obviously a fine physical specimen.

But the Lord said to Samuel,

> Do not look at his appearance or at his physical stature, because I have refused him. For the Lord does not see as man sees; for man looks at the outward appearance, but the Lord looks at the heart (1 Samuel 16:7).

Earlier in 1 Samuel 13, Samuel had told Saul that Saul had acted foolishly and not kept the commandment of the Lord. Therefore, Samuel went on to tell Saul that the Lord had found a "man after His own heart" to be commander over His people. We know that man was David, the youngest son of Jesse.

What made David a man after God's own heart? We read in 1 Kings 15:5 that God was going to set up David's son, Solomon, as king and establish Jerusalem "because David did what was right in the eyes of the Lord, and had not turned aside from anything that He commanded him all the days of his life, except in the matter of Uriah the Hittite."

There are two things we need to note here. David did what was right in the eyes of the Lord and had not turned aside from anything that God commanded him, with one exception, all the days of his life.

Does that tell us that David was an almost perfect human being? We know that David had idols in his house (1 Samuel 19:13–16). We know that he lied to the priest, Ahimelech, in 1 Samuel 21. David displayed a temper in 1 Samuel 25:21–22 and had multiple wives (1 Samuel 25). David took another man's wife and then had her husband killed (2 Samuel 11). We learn in subsequent chapters that his children were out of control. One has to wonder how David could be a man after God's own heart.

We need only to look at David's attitude to understand what God desires of us. We need to be able to see the unseen. David's redeeming virtue was his consuming penitent response to knowing that he had sinned against God. We are told that David understood that the "sacrifices of God are a broken spirit, a broken and a contrite heart" (Psalm 51:17).

Many times in the Psalms we are told that David walked in integrity. He mentions that God upheld his integrity (Psalm 41:12). *The Theological Dictionary* by Rahner and Vorgrimler says of integrity:

> In the sphere of morals, integrity primarily means the physiological and psychological completeness of man, of which no "part" may become independent (as in the voluntary or morbid dominance of a particular impulse), or which may be interfered with only so far as the good of the organism may require (medical intervention): in moral theology integrity means the integration of a whole human being into a fundamental option that is morally good.

In David's case, his integrity was upheld because he desired what God wanted of him. He lived in this world as a normal, physical human being, but his heart, in essence, belonged to God.

We are reminded of the apostle Paul who said, "For me to live is Christ." As much as I love my husband and my family, I know that "for me to live is Christ." No matter what else happens in our lives—whatever sadness, whatever loss, whatever joy, whatever goodness—we must understand that in order to be spiritually beautiful we have to know that for us "to live is Christ." Just as David was a man after God's own heart, so should we be seeking the will of our Father and living with integrity, knowing that we have eternity set in our hearts.

Go back and read the definition of integrity as defined in the *Theological Dictionary*. If we "shuck the corn and show the cob" of that definition, the meaning of integrity is "non-hypocritical." Integrity means living a transparent life.

David lived a transparent life. In Psalm 51:1, David cried out for mercy. Notice that he did not ask for justice. He knew that he had sinned against God and that if justice were to be administered he had every reason to die. He needed the mercy of God just as each one of us does. When we realize that need for the mercy of God every day of our lives, we are coming close to having the kind of heart God requires

> *"All things are naked and open to the eyes of Him to whom we must give account."*
> *—Hebrews 4:13*

of us. May we never respond to the Lord like the Pharisee in Luke 18:11–12 who prayed, "God, I thank You that I am not like other men—extortioners, unjust, adulterers, or even as this tax collector. I fast twice a week; I give tithes of all that I possess."

But rather, may we respond like the tax collector "standing afar off, [who] would not so much as raise his eyes to heaven, but beat his breast, saying 'God, be merciful to me a sinner!' " A broken and contrite heart realizes that it needs the mercy of God, just as David and the tax collector did.

Also, we notice in Psalms 51 that David made no excuses for his sin. He used the words *transgression, iniquity,* and *evil.* We hardly recognize those words in our culture today. We might have used the words "no recollection," a "sickness," a "genetic disorder," a "dependent personality," or an "alternative lifestyle" and expect that to be acceptable to our Lord.

David built no meticulous defense. He knew what he had done and he knew that God knew. He knew that his life was transparent before God. A spiritually beautiful woman knows that, too. She may sin, and will sin, but she knows that those sins are not hidden from God. She does understand, however, that her sins are blotted out by the blood of Christ and that when Christ appears in glory she will too (Colossians 3:3–4).

David obviously wanted to stand clean before God and he asked God to blot out his sin and to cleanse him. Only when we can say with David, "Create in me a pure heart," and give to God our broken and contrite heart can He give to us an inward spiritual renewal.

Let us look at two women in the New Testament who demonstrated two different heart responses to the Lord. The first woman is Sapphira, the wife of Ananias, in Acts 5. Sapphira obviously had heard the word of God. She and her husband had sold a field and conspired together to say that they were giving all of the money they had received from the sale of the field to the Lord. Three hours after Ananias had been stricken dead for lying to Peter, Sapphira came before Peter. He asked her, "Tell me whether you sold the land for so much?" And she answered, "Yes, for so much."

Then Peter said to her, "How is it that you have agreed together to test the Spirit of the Lord? Look, the feet of those who have buried your husband are at the door, and they will carry you out."

What was Sapphira's sin? Her sin was in not living a transparent life before her Lord. It was saying one thing and doing another. It was believing that she could hide something from God. In this case, she was really not hiding a sin; her sin was lying about the truth. I am convinced that Sapphira would not have been required to give every dime she had made on the sale of the field to God. She just wanted everyone to think that she had.

In our lives today it is easy for us to want others to think that we are spiritual. We may be at every service of the church, properly dressed and in a quiet spirit, but if a tape recorder were left on in our homes, the world would see another side of us. We must never make the mistake that Sapphira made. The tape recorder runs 24 hours a day, 7 days a week. God knows.

Now let us look at another woman who exemplifies the truly transparent heart. She was willing just to be one of the "little dogs." She is found in Mark 7 and is a priceless example for us.

> For a woman whose young daughter had an unclean spirit heard about Him, and she came and fell at his feet. The woman was a Greek, A Syro-Phoenician by birth, and she kept asking him to cast the demon out of her daughter. But Jesus said to her, "Let the children be filled first, for it is not good to take the children's bread and throw it to the little dogs." And she answered and said, "Yes, Lord, yet even the little dogs under the table eat from the children's crumbs" (Mark 7:25–28).

We know that when she returned home that Jesus had sent the demon out of her daughter. Why? Because of the purity of this woman's heart. I can't help but think that Jesus must have looked at her and loved her for her transparency.

We want God to know us as women after His own heart. Walking in integrity and living a transparent life means living by the words of God no matter what it costs. It means being the same person in a bad situation that you are in a good situation. It means not lying about your age or the age of your child to save two dollars or two thousand dollars. It means not taking a contract for your construction company if you are being hired to build an abortion clinic. It means taking responsibility when you have made a mistake. It means calling sin, sin. A woman after God's own heart is able to say, "Create in me a pure heart." Then she lives her life allowing God to do that. It is being willing to be one of the "little dogs," knowing that you live with a pure heart in the presence of God daily.

Questions for Discussion

1. Why do you think Samuel thought that God's anointed was before Him when he saw Eliab?

2. What did God tell Samuel was the difference in what Samuel saw and what God saw? Why is that important for us to remember today?

3. What had Saul done that caused God to give the kingdom to David?

4. How will a person with a "heart after God's own heart" respond to the commandments of God? Refer to 1 Samuel 13:14; 1 Kings 15:5; and John 14:15.

5. What is meant by having integrity? How can we have integrity in our everyday lives? How will the Lord uphold us in our integrity as He did David?

6. How can we be sure that we can stand clean in God's sight? Why is it dangerous to live in a society that makes excuses for sin? What words do Christians use that make sin seem more acceptable?

7. What was Sapphira's sin?

8. What was the Syro-Phoenician woman's redeeming quality? Compare her to Sapphira.

9. How can we live a transparent life in Christ? How will our doing so encourage others?

10. Why is it so hard for us to truly experience a broken and contrite heart when it comes to our spiritual lives. How does 1 Corinthians 10:12 relate to your answer?

Chapter 13

⟨⊚⟩⟨⊚⟩

"The Whole Ball of Wax"

"Now godliness with contentment
is great gain."
— 1 Timothy 6:6—

After teaching a seminar recently, a precious older sister—who, I later learned, had been the preacher's wife at that congregation for over 20 years—came up to me, patted my hand, and said, "Godliness with contentment, honey."

I smiled. "That's the whole ball of wax, isn't it?" I asked.

"Yes, honey," she answered. "The whole ball of wax!"

So what is godliness? Hopefully, in the previous chapters of this book you have begun to understand that spiritual beauty equates to godliness. Do you remember in Exodus, chapter 3, when Moses decided to go and see the burning bush? As he approached the bush, God told him, "Do not draw near this place. Take your sandals off your feet, for the place where you stand is holy ground."

Do you think that particular piece of ground was any different from the rest of the ground around the area? What made it holy ground?

What made it holy ground was the presence of God. It is the very same thing that makes us holy. Living our physical lives on this earth daily in the presence of God with a pure heart is holiness. Holiness is spiritual beauty.

We are told in Genesis 5:22–24 that Enoch walked with God. We also know that Noah walked with God (Genesis 6:9). What does it mean to walk with God?

Have you ever invited someone to take a walk with you? It was probably because you enjoy their company. Most of the time when you walk with someone for any length of time it becomes an intimate time. You share things. You talk to the other person and the other person talks to you.

In order to walk with God in this life, one would certainly talk to Him. Walking with God today would include a very vibrant prayer life. It would also include letting God talk to us through His Word, while sincerely listening to what He has to say. That would mean studying His Word and knowing more than just a few verses out of context. It would include knowing God.

> *"Enoch walked with God, and he was not, for God took him."*
> —*Genesis 5:24*

Make no mistake about this: How we spend our minutes, how we spend our hours, and how we spend our days is how we are spending our lives. As hard as it is for us to comprehend on a minute-by-minute, hour-by-hour, day-by-day basis, each one of us is laying down our life for something every single day. Is it our job? Is it our family? Is it our house? Or is it our God?

Whether we live to be 30, 50, 70, or 100 years old, at the end this life will have been short. Ask any older person. They will tell you that the years fly even faster as one ages. Our life certainly is a vapor as we are told in James, chapter 4. One vapor may be more dense than another and take longer to dissipate, but all vapor will vanish.

When each of us walks individually—and we will walk individually—through the valley of the shadow, what thoughts will fill our minds? We surely will not be wishing we had spent more time at the office, done more housework, or watched more T.V. But will we have let those things keep us from having walked in this life with our God?

In truth, our very last breath should be taken in our very finest hour. We will finally be going to be with our Lord. If we have spent a great deal of time with Him on this earth, we will be going to meet our Creator and our very best Friend.

We read in the Scriptures how we can abide in Christ: "Now he who keeps His commandments abides in Him, and He in him. And by this we know that He abides in us, by the Spirit whom He has given us" (1 John 3:24). God has given us the means to know if we are abiding in Him. There should be no question in your life. If there is, then you need to saturate your life with the promises of God. God will do what He says He will do if we do what He asks us to do.

The story is told of a young preacher, fresh out of college, who was going to visit an elderly gentleman who did not have long to live. The young preacher agonized over what words of comfort and assurance he could give the older gentleman. As the young preacher was getting ready to leave, he really felt as if he had not been much of a comfort to the man. He just had not known what to say. After he prayed with the older gentleman, he turned to leave, and as he opened the screen door to the front porch, his own little dog, who had followed him, came bounding into the room and jumped into his arms. The young preacher smiled. He turned to the older gentleman.

"Did you see my dog run into this room?" he asked.

The older man nodded.

"He has never been to your house before. He has certainly never been in this room before. But look how happy he was to come in that door and into this room. Do you know why? Because his master is here. And you, my dear friend, will be even happier to pass from this life and into the next to meet the Master whom you have served so faithfully in this life!" At that moment, a smile crossed the elderly man's face.

A few days ago I was in the front yard working and realized that I was wearing a 50-dollar silk blouse. The reason I was wearing it to do yard work was because I had a hard time remembering that it was a 50-dollar blouse. Why? Because I had paid only 10 dollars for it!

I am convinced that the value that we place on our relationship to the Lord and, consequently, our spiritual beauty will be a direct result of how much it has cost us.

A few months ago I decided to make strawberry ice cream. Usually when making ice cream, I just throw in the ingredients and hope it turns out good. Sometimes we have a milkshake. I have never been one to measure precisely. However, this time I had paid a lot for the strawberries and I wanted the ice cream to be really good. So I followed a recipe that I had tasted before. I have to tell you that I went exactly by that recipe. I measured every ingredient exactly. I beat it just the right amount of time. And guess what? The ice cream turned out wonderfully. (Amazing how that works, isn't it?)

After dinner I set a bowl of the ice cream in front of my husband for dessert. After 30 years of being married to him, I knew what he would say. A few minutes later when I was standing in front of the dishwasher loading dishes, I heard him yell into the kitchen, "You did good, Ma!"

That is exactly what I knew he would say. However, in the same instant I thought of the people in Matthew 25 who heard the Lord say, "Well, done, thou good and faithful servant," and I wondered what it would be like listening for Him to say that to me one day. What will it be like listening for God to call *my* name?

Our goal in seeking spiritual beauty should be to hear the Lord say, "Well done, thou good and faithful servant." In order for that to happen we need to follow the recipe. We need to know the Word of God and we need to live the Word of God.

Let us hear the conclusion of the whole matter: Fear God and keep His commandments, for this is man's all. For God will bring every work into judgment, including every secret thing, whether good or evil (Ecclesiastes 12:13–14).

That's the whole ball of wax!

Questions for Discussion

1. Why was Moses told to take his shoes off in Exodus 3?

2. What made the ground holy?

3. How can we walk with God in our own lives today?

4. Do you believe that each one of us is laying down our life for something every day? How can we make sure that we are living *with* and *for* our God? What changes do some need to make in order to do that?

5. How is it that each one of us walks individually in the valley of the shadow?

6. Why should our last breath be our finest hour?

7. How can one abide in Christ?

8. According to the author, how much will we value our relationship with the Lord?

9. What does the author imply about following the recipe in our lives? How does this relate to our spiritual beauty?

10. Why do you think the value of our relationship with the Lord will be a direct correlation to how much it has cost us?

11. What is the conclusion of the whole matter? Will we be different from the world when we understand this? How? In what ways?

v